10%
BRAVER

Sara Miller McCune founded SAGE Publishing in 1965 to support the dissemination of usable knowledge and educate a global community. SAGE publishes more than 1000 journals and over 800 new books each year, spanning a wide range of subject areas. Our growing selection of library products includes archives, data, case studies and video. SAGE remains majority owned by our founder and after her lifetime will become owned by a charitable trust that secures the company's continued independence.

Los Angeles | London | New Delhi | Singapore | Washington DC | Melbourne

edited by

VIVIENNE PORRITT
KEZIAH FEATHERSTONE

10%
BRAVER

INSPIRING WOMEN TO LEAD EDUCATION

#WomenEd

Los Angeles | London | New Delhi
Singapore | Washington DC | Melbourne

Los Angeles | London | New Delhi
Singapore | Washington DC | Melbourne

SAGE Publications Ltd
1 Oliver's Yard
55 City Road
London EC1Y 1SP

SAGE Publications Inc.
2455 Teller Road
Thousand Oaks, California 91320

SAGE Publications India Pvt Ltd
B 1/I 1 Mohan Cooperative Industrial Area
Mathura Road
New Delhi 110 044

SAGE Publications Asia-Pacific Pte Ltd
3 Church Street
#10-04 Samsung Hub
Singapore 049483

Publisher: James Clark
Assistant editor: Diana Alves
Production editor: Nicola Carrier
Copyeditor: Chris Bitten
Proofreader: Leigh C. Smithson
Indexer: Silvia Benvenuto
Marketing manager: Dilhara Attygalle
Cover design: Wendy Scott
Typeset by: C&M Digitals (P) Ltd, Chennai, India
Printed in the UK

Editorial arrangement © Vivienne Porritt and
Keziah Featherstone 2019
Chapter 1 © Hannah Wilson 2019
Chapter 2 © Sue Cowley 2019
Chapter 3 © Jules Daulby 2019
Chapter 4 © Liz Free 2019
Chapter 5 © Sameena Choudry 2019
Chapter 6 © Angela Browne 2019
Chapter 7 © Claire Nicholls 2019
Chapter 8 © Jill Berry 2019
Chapter 9 © Chris Hildrew 2019
Chapter 10 © Helena Marsh and Caroline Derbyshire 2019
Chapter 11 © Vivienne Porritt 2019
Chapter 12 © Keziah Featherstone 2019

First published 2019

Library of Congress Control Number: 2018953035

British Library Cataloguing in Publication data

A catalogue record for this book is available from
the British Library

ISBN 978-1-5264-6003-5
ISBN 978-1-5264-6004-2 (pbk)

At SAGE we take sustainability seriously. Most of our products are printed in the UK using responsibly sourced
papers and boards. When we print overseas we ensure sustainable papers are used as measured by the PREPS
grading system. We undertake an annual audit to monitor our sustainability.

TABLE OF CONTENTS

ABOUT THE EDITORS

Vivienne Porritt is a leadership consultant and works with school and academy trust leaders on impact, vision, strategy, professional learning and development, and leadership, especially women's leadership. Vivienne is the co-editor of *Effective Practices in CPD, Lessons for School* (2009). She is on the editorial board of *School Leadership and Management*, and is a coach for the Department for Education. Formerly she was a secondary headteacher, and Director for School Partnerships at UCL Institute of Education as well as a Chair of Governors in London. Vivienne is delighted to be a Founding Fellow of the Chartered College of Teaching. Vivienne is also a co-founder and, joyously, one of the national leaders of #WomenEd.

Keziah Featherstone is currently head at Q3 Academy Tipton, having previously been head at an all-through school in Bristol. She is a co-founder and national leader for #WomenEd, a member of the Headteachers' Roundtable and writes for several educational publications. She likes to nap.

ABOUT THE CONTRIBUTORS

Jill Berry taught in six schools across a 30-year career and was a head for the last ten, the job she loved more than any other. Since finishing headship she has completed a doctorate, written 'Making the Leap – Moving from deputy to head', and worked as a leadership development consultant.

Angela Browne is the Deputy CEO of a multi-academy trust near Bristol. She is also an Education Leadership Coach who coaches and supports educators so they can bring authentic, grounded leadership to their teams. She is passionate about diversity, creating schools in which everyone flourishes, and the power of education.

Sameena Choudry is the founder of Equitable Education and co-founder and National Leader of #WomenEd. Sameena has experience as a teacher, lecturer, ITE tutor, examiner, senior leader, adviser and in senior officer roles as well as being a trained Ofsted inspector. Her consultancy work focuses on significantly improving standards of attainment for pupils previously under-attaining.

Sue Cowley is a writer, teacher and author of 30 education books. Her book *Getting the Buggers to Behave* has been translated into ten languages. She has written for the *Tes*, *Teach Primary* and *Nursery World*. Sue works internationally as a teacher trainer and helps to run her local preschool.

Jules Daulby is a national leader of #WomenEd and a feminist, campaigning for gender equality and balance. Jules is dedicated to social equity and comprehensive education. She lives in Dorset with her husband and four children. Jules began teaching in 1998 as an English and Drama teacher, then Deputy Head of sixth form before having a two year break in the Falkland Islands as a radio news broadcaster. Since then, she has specialised in literacy and mainstream special educational needs.

Caroline Derbyshire is CEO of Saffron Academy Trust, a MAT of two secondaries and four primaries in North Essex. She is an NLE, a mother of two and a #WomenEd Leadership Mentor. Caroline is an elected member of the Headteacher Board for the North-East London and East of England Region.

Liz Free is the Director of the International Leadership Academy in The Hague. With extensive UK and international education experience, she is a passionate advocate for developing school leadership. Liz is the co-founder and leader of #WomenEdNL and is mum to the suitably inquisitive Freya and Austin.

Chris Hildrew started teaching English in the East Midlands after graduating from New College, Oxford. He moved to the South West in 2010 as Deputy Headteacher at Chew Valley School, before landing his dream role as Headteacher of Churchill Academy & Sixth Form, in North Somerset, in January 2016.

Helena Marsh is Executive Principal of CHET Multi Academy Trust and Principal of Linton Village College. Helena is a Specialist Leader of Education and published author. Her expertise includes professional learning, school culture, teacher collaboration, workload and relational schools. Helena is a co-founder of #WomenEd and a member of the Headteachers' Roundtable.

Claire Nicholls has been teaching for ten years. After a Primary PGCE, she found her passion in Special Educational Needs teaching and has led inclusion in mainstream and specialist settings. She is currently a SENDCo at a secondary school in Bristol and a Specialist Leader in Education for SEND.

Hannah Wilson is the Executive Headteacher of Aureus School and Aureus Primary School, part of the GLF Schools Trust. She is the Strategic Lead for the GLF Teaching School Alliance and the Sub-regional Strategic Lead for the SE Women Leading in Education Network for Oxon, Berks and Bucks (NCTL). Hannah co-founded #WomenEd and was a National Leader for #WomenEd until September 2018. She is a DfE coach for the Women Leading in Education initiative. Hannah is also a Trustee for the GEMs Primary Academies in Didcot and Twickenham.

ACKNOWLEDGEMENTS

Without Jules, Sameena, Hannah, Helena and Natalie, there would be no #WomenEd and this book would not exist, so thank you co-founders for your determination and foresight. Without thousands of women and men across the globe, there would not be a dynamic and incredible movement to inspire this book. Without a shadow of a doubt, James Clark and Diana Alves at SAGE have made this book come into being, along with the whole editorial, marketing and production team: we hope we live up to expectations. Lastly, the wonderful words of all chapter authors and contributors represent the #WomenEd community beautifully, so thanks to you.

Keziah would especially like to acknowledge the love and support of her family and friends – particularly Andy, Evie, mum and dad. The creation of this book coincided with some dark days; I will be eternally grateful to all those in the #WomenEd community who supported me at this time. Still I rise.

Vivienne would especially like to thank Tony and Julie for their patience and love and my family and friends who always support me. Thank you also to the wonderful #WomenEd community who lifted me up when I faced adversity and who continue to make me hopeful and proud. Still we rise.

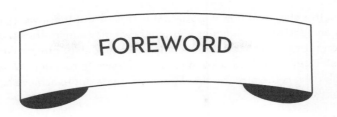

FOREWORD

When I read the proof copy of this book, I tweeted that I believed it was powerful enough to be a 'game-changer'. Within moments, a chorus of encouragement embraced me from Twitter echoing, liking, adding to my tweet. The process of reading the voices of so many women sang to me and, as I read, I could feel my own professional courage increase. #WomenEd embodies the promise of collective endeavour and collegiality. This is a movement that achieved almost overnight recognition and support from thousands of colleagues within education (mainly but not exclusively women). Before our eyes, within a short space of time, #WomenEd has emerged onto the educational landscape with refreshing warmth and humour but with a steely determination to challenge inequity relentlessly.

Throughout my career in education I have tried to follow the path least travelled. I have allowed my heart to influence career choices and passion for an alternative improvement agenda to inspire energy even at times of near exhaustion. Always, throughout, I have loved the transformative effect of teaching. As a headteacher, I became completely immersed in the world of our school. The successes of children, staff and wider community members became a shared success. Research into *Learning without Limits* focused on the importance of 'finding a way through' collectively to support and inspire achievement beyond what others may expect. Everything that I believe is educationally important is embodied within this inclusive approach. Refusing to accept limits, defying labels, embracing struggle – all of this is also utterly at the centre of #WomenEd.

Sometimes in life there are times when stepping forward, being 10% braver, is more compelling than waiting for others to act. In 2016, in partnership with Julie Lilly, we created a Twitter storm about assessment, resulting in a series of events across the country offering a pedagogy for principled assessment under the banner #BeyondLevels. The willingness of colleagues to share practice, to support innovation and to encourage others to be courageous that we witnessed at these events offered new hope for professionalism and the future of education. Working together with #WomenEd, the newly formed Chartered College of Teaching seeks to build on the power of networks with agency for change to create a profession-led system that is ethical and driven by core notions of equity, diversity and ambition for all.

This book matters because it is guaranteed to inspire, to educate and to spark a much-needed clamour for women to assume roles of influence throughout our education system. When I was appointed to the role of Chief Executive of the Chartered College of Teaching I freely admit that I faced a huge challenge. The easier role would have been to stay in school, leave it to others to lead, watch from the sidelines . . . It takes guts to push for change, but the reality is that when we begin to work together everything gets easier and seems possible. Hope, vision and collaboration encourage previously unknown strength.

What bursts out of these pages is the power of the collective. We need this at scale and we need it more than ever. Passive acceptance of injustice, inequity and prejudice is hard to challenge in isolation, but change becomes possible and real through the power of communities. Within each chapter every author celebrates the story of a personal role model. These inspirational vignettes show just how important it is to seek out those we can learn from, both within the family and amongst colleagues and others we may admire from a distance. Reading this book, inspired to action, you too can become a role model for others. We are reminded of the importance of living our values, allowing our inner voice to recognise what is possible and acting accordingly. That is the promise that #WomenEd sets out to achieve and achieve it they will, with your help. Go to it.

ALISON PEACOCK
CHIEF EXECUTIVE OF THE CHARTERED COLLEGE OF TEACHING

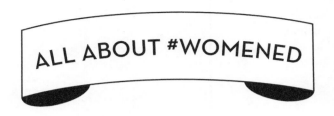

ALL ABOUT #WOMENED

GETTING INVOLVED WITH WOMENED

We hope we have inspired you to engage with #WomenEd, and one of the best ways to do this is to go to an event. Our events are posted on Eventbrite and shared on our social media sites, our app and our website. Here are ways you can contact or connect with us:

Twitter   @WomenEd is our main Twitter account. Our hashtag is #WomenEd, which we use for all our events and networking so you can engage with what is happening across our global networks. Search for @WomenEd on Twitter and a list of our networks appears.

Blog   womenedblog.wordpress.com Our blog is a great place to engage in debate, dialogue, reflection and celebration.

Facebook   You can also engage with us here: facebook.com/womened

Website   womened.org

Newsletter   https://mailchi.mp/2eec9d3558fa/womened

App   App store: buff.ly/2dHEqo4 (*Our app is a work in progress*)
Google play: buff.ly/2dHDjoj

Email   womenedleaders@gmail.com

Eventbrite   Eventbrite.co.uk Search for #WomenEd and a location.

Periscope   Some events are recorded: search for #WomenEd via the Periscope app.

Thanks to Pen Mendonça, who has created graphic recordings of our events as well as the amazing image of our #WomenEd values in Chapter 1.

Pen Mendonça is a pioneering graphic facilitator with 20 years' experience of working across the UK public and voluntary sectors, and directly with communities. Her essays can be found in *Studies in Comics, Women: A Cultural Review* and Demeter Press books on motherhood. Her Twitter name is @MendoncaPen

1

#WOMENED: OUR STORY AND OUR VALUES

HANNAH WILSON

KEY POINTS

This chapter will outline:

- Why #WomenEd had to exist

- How #WomenEd came into being

- How we created our shared values, the 8Cs, and what they mean in practice

- Who is who in the #WomenEd story

INTRODUCTION

From a hashtag to a global movement, our small group of women didn't know what we were starting when we first communicated on Twitter. Relative strangers, we arranged to meet for afternoon tea to discuss our passion for gender equality, our concerns about the gender gap in our profession, and what we could do collectively to make a difference.

Since this most English of traditions, #WomenEd has engaged with over twenty thousand educators and gathered momentum across the UK and the wider world. The success of our community stems from our shared vision and values and our determination to improve education. The power of a grassroots movement should never be underestimated.

CONTEXT

Despite spending our whole careers knowing gender equality in educational leadership was an issue, it was the publication, in February 2015, of research by the Future Leaders Trust that really hit home. We learned that:

- The school workforce in England was 74% female, yet only 65% of headteachers were women
- If these percentages were equal, there would be over 1,500 more female headteachers in the UK
- The issue is far more prevalent in secondary schools: 38% of the workforce were male and 62% were female. But when you look at headteachers, the numbers are reversed: just 36% were women (Future Leaders Trust, 2015)

Those of us meeting for tea that afternoon wanted to do more than just challenge the deficit in the number of female headteachers compared to the number of female teachers in our schools. Our goal was much bigger than that. Together we were determined to break and reshape the leadership mould to enable a different type of leader to develop, thrive and succeed in the teaching profession. Together we wanted to make our schools more family friendly and our profession more people-centred. By challenging the system and creating choice, we wanted to improve and increase leadership opportunities for all.

VALUES

Vision and values are central to effective leadership. #WomenEd models how to find your why, articulate your values, engage your stakeholders and how to affect change as an individual, as an organisation and in a system. In many ways we did things in the wrong order when we launched, but none of us anticipated how quickly the movement would pick up pace nor how large we would grow. In retrospect, we should have nailed down our mission, vision and values from the outset, but we only framed these when we were seven months old when Vivienne Porritt and I pulled together common threads from our discussions and events. We reflected on what resonated with our followers and where we found synergy. These were the foundations of the 8Cs. Although we were aware we were approaching world domination backwards, this approach did enable us to represent our audience and reflect back the ideas and language we had heard since our conception.

An early focus point for discussions was Staffrm, a short-lived but well-loved blogging site, where contributors detailed the barriers women in education were facing. It provided a platform for confessing the fear of failure and tips on how to manage imposter syndrome and quieten 'the inner critic'. This collaborative approach, made possible by social media and crowd-sourcing perspectives, led to the articulation of our #WomenEd values. With everything happening in the world, we need values-led leaders more than ever.

We fondly abbreviate our values to the 8Cs. They underpin our community and are a call to arms for the movement:

Clarity: Acknowledge the gender imbalance in education leadership

Communication: Actively seek to promote the #WomenEd mission

Connection: Connect existing and aspiring leaders and those who support them

Community: Create an inclusive and interactive community

Confidence: Take opportunities to be #10% braver

Collaboration: Enhance collaboration and sharing of experience

Challenge: Highlight systemic barriers to more inclusive and diverse leadership

Change: Collate evidence of impact on developing inclusive and diverse leadership

#WomenEdLondon #LeadMeet March, 2017, graphics by MendoncaPen

Figure 1.1 #WomenEd's 8Cs

I often use the 8Cs to work through a problem or to build an argument. Let's take flexible working as an example: there are 250,000 qualified teachers in the UK who are currently not working in our schools, so if we could make our schools more family friendly we could perhaps encourage them back into the classroom. If we welcomed them to a #WomenEd event they could meet a coach, find a role model and connect with another group like Maternity CPD (@maternityCPD). Through coaching, the individual would feel more confident to apply for a role and might go on to ask for flexible working. Together, we can change the lives of children who need a teacher and the career of a teacher who otherwise might have left the sector. In the UK, national media may be calling it a 'recruitment crisis', but it would be more accurate to say that we have a 'retention crisis' in our schools. The largest demographic leaving our profession are women in their thirties, women who are having the choice made for them: work full time or you cannot be a leader, lead like a man or stay as a teacher, work full time or find another school.

VISION

The #WomenEd vision will vary for everyone in our community, dependent on their own experience and context, yet there are some common solutions to barriers to improve the system for everyone. 'Authentic leadership' means being yourself, finding where you fit and celebrating the diversity of our schools. Nurturing the confidence of women in education is vital to ensure we put ourselves forward for opportunities, that we bounce back when we experience failure and, moreover, that we know our non-negotiables and where we are not prepared to compromise. With confidence comes a sense of self-worth and strength to ask for what we need, be that negotiating flexible working or increased salaries. If we empower the women in the system, invest in them and recognise their potential, then we will more likely retain them.

MISSION

Our mission is to empower more women in education to have *the choice* to progress on their leadership journey.

#WomenEd is not an organisation that strives to have quantitative measures to analyse. We are not a movement to get more women to be headteachers, though we celebrate when that happens. Instead we are about people, relationships, storytelling and their impact. We are a community of change makers who have agency, a shared vision and a collective voice. When we first started tweeting we were a small quiet voice; four years later we are a roar of more than twenty thousand voices. We are being consulted on policies that can bring about systemic change for the future of our schools and our colleagues.

For women, progressing through their careers is not always a linear journey. We cross-traverse our careers, stepping on and off around our personal lives. As Sheryl Sandberg, in her book *Lean In*, calls it, our careers resemble a 'jungle gym' (2013: 53). For us it is about having the choice or realising that there are barriers that prevent and inhibit us from progressing. #WomenEd is the sledgehammer that smashes the glass ceiling. It is the choice of the individual whether they want to climb through that hole or not.

CLARITY

In Spring 2015, Helena Marsh wrote a popular blog entitled: 'What glass ceiling?' (Marsh, 2017). Jill Berry, a retired headteacher, penned a reply entitled 'The lost leaders', those who could have been 'exceptional leaders and role models but who, for a variety of reasons, didn't fulfil their leadership potential' (Berry, 2017). The two blogs generated a lot of tweets and reflection. Natalie Scott (then Assistant Headteacher on the Isle of Wight), Vivienne Porritt (then Director of the Institute of Education's London Centre for Leadership in Learning and a Chair of Governors) and I (then a Deputy Headteacher in London) spent all weekend in the throng of a heated debate. We were adamant that there was a glass ceiling for women in education, especially those who wanted to both lead and have a family. Jules Daulby (then a Special Educational Needs Coordinator (SENCO) in Dorset), Keziah Featherstone (then a headteacher in Bristol) and Sameena Choudry, an educational diversity consultant from Doncaster, joined the conversation. Collectively we agreed that we needed to harness the passion and interest that this debate had sparked, and Keziah suggested that we should have 'a little conference' (Porritt, 2017). Vivienne collated the ideas and offers of support in a third blog, and asked whether people wanted to join in. Then it exploded with over three thousand views of that blog and its successor. To us, this suggested that women in education who are or who aspire to be leaders need our voices to be heard and to connect with each other to support our aspirations.

To meet in person was our natural next step. On a Sunday afternoon in May 2015, seven strangers met for afternoon tea at a hotel near Bracknell with Sameena joining us on Skype: a weird and wonderful place for a grassroots movement to start! We found common ground quickly – who knew we would all be secondary English teachers – and bonded as a team.

As Margaret Mead says in a quote we all love: 'It takes a small group of committed individuals to change the world.' Four years on, we are getting closer to it.

An idea. A name. A Twitter handle. A hashtag. A logo. An abundance of passion and energy. A grassroots movement was born. A community was started.

Figure 1.2 The #WomenEd logo

Our name causes contention and we are aware that it isn't grammatically correct! We wanted a name that did what it said on the tin: a movement *by* women in education *for* women in education, a platform to give an emerging audience voice and agency, a community to amplify the experiences and stories of women in education. 'It was never a dress!' is another quote that we love. Our figures are not in dresses but in sheroes' capes. The microphone symbolises us finding and using our voices and amplifying the voices of others. Purple has become synonymous with our community and events, a homage to the colours of the suffragettes and suffragists. Thank you to my former colleague, Rob Webb, who designed the logo for us.

We wanted to plan an event to bring those who were interested in contributing together to continue the online discussions, but we all had full-time jobs and we didn't have any funds. My tweet asking for ideas for funding had a reply by Philip Montague, who was then in the Small Medium Enterprise team at Microsoft UK. He kindly offered to give us a venue for the event free of charge.

Was it really going to be that easy? Seemingly it was. Within weeks we had a central London location, a date, and we were inundated with offers to facilitate workshops at our inaugural grassroots event.

COMMUNICATION

The Staffrm blogging community for educators and tweachers (teachers who tweet) was instrumental in our journey as a grassroots movement. The #WomenEd #DigiMeet (a digital meet up) became a regular feature with a Sunday of themed blogging. Many of our established #WomenEd contributors found their voice on Twitter, extended their reflections on Staffrm and have since launched their own blogs. Pre and post #WomenEd event blogs enabled the community to continue the discussions and deepen the reflections. This safe space was quite sacred for us. In Autumn 2017, the National Leaders decided to launch a #WomenEd blog (https://womened blog.wordpress.com/), curated by Keziah, to maintain a platform to support women in blogging and continue to amplify our voices.

It is through the blogs and our events that we cascade strategies and ideas using a method called 'the illumination technique'. This has its roots in US politics, where a group of women working in the White House devised a plan to reinforce and echo great ideas and to attribute them back to the rightful owners (Landsbaum, 2016).

CONNECTION

To connect women leaders a step further, we set up our annual unconference to establish ourselves as a grassroots movement. An unconference is a more open and democratic type of event that is driven by participants and avoids top-down, hierarchical approaches. This choice was a deliberate move away from the male-dominated education events with all-male panels and experts telling others what to do. At our inaugural unconference in September 2015, over 60 facilitators shared their knowledge and successes while also participating as one of the 200 delegates at the unconference. Our events are not about speakers rocking up, presenting and leaving, but about being a part of a community. This peer-led approach flattened the leadership hierarchy that has become so isolating in our schools and sees new teachers sitting next to and developing professional friendships with CEOs.

COMMUNITY

Our growth from a community of seven to over twenty thousand is indicative of the need of women leaders to be connected and supported. We realised quite quickly that we had taken on a much bigger project than we had anticipated. Two of our co-founders (Helena Marsh and Natalie Scott) stepped back from leading our strategy due to other commitments and Jules Daulby, Keziah Featherstone, Sameena Choudry, Vivienne Porritt and myself continued. Due to my workload, I stepped down as a National Leader after our fourth unconference in 2018, with Jules, Keziah, Sameena and Vivienne continuing as National Leaders who support the grassroots movement to grow. Already overwhelmed with interest and invites, we proceeded to recruit volunteers to join us.

We tweeted out in November 2015 that we were seeking volunteers to grow the network locally. By our first birthday in April 2016, we had announced 40 Regional Leaders who connected and collaborated in regional hubs across the country. We now have more than 80 volunteers who generously give their time and energy to help us arrange face-to-face events for our community. The purpose of our Regional Teams is to distribute the leadership of the #WomenEd mission and they represent the diversity of our sector. Grassroots movements are by the people, for the people, just like this book is by members of the #WomenEd community for women in education.

As with any induction, we meet with new Regional Leaders via face-to-face or online orientation sessions to align visions and values and to develop team relationships. Leading virtually is a different skill set and we have learned a great deal about how we connect, communicate and collaborate.

To ensure our approach stays true to our values we created a set of reflections, discussions and activities, framed by our 8Cs, for each regional group to use to align us all. The following questions are a sample of these:

1. How do we ensure an inclusive, diverse, collaborative regional community?
2. What does sharing leadership experience look like?
3. How do we build on existing social media presence?
4. How do we reach beyond social media?
5. How do we develop the connections and conversations across the region?
6. How do we identify and meet the needs of women leaders at all levels?
7. How do we have impact?
8. How do we capture the difference we make?

We based our community infrastructure on the Department for Education regions. Each of the National Leaders are attached to Regional Networks to support and ensure consistency across the country, and to ensure communication. For example, I supported the teams in the West Midlands and the East Midlands: we have ten volunteers in each region and tended to operate as a team of 20!

CONFIDENCE

Sue Cowley (an experienced early years teacher, and the best-selling author of over 25 books for educators) was a natural choice as our opening contributor at our inaugural #WomenEd unconference. She embodies our values as someone who champions change and challenges the system. In her presentation, which included her singing some of Helen Reddy's song 'I am Woman', she shared a conversation with an old friend about courage, and our movement's mantra of being 10% Braver was born. Sue talks about this in detail in Chapter 2 of this book. The sporting 'marginal gains' theory was cited for the success of the Great Britain cycling team at the London 2012 Olympics. Well, 10% Braver is like that and has led to so many stories of personal and professional change effected by pushing ourselves gently out of our comfort zones: it motivates us to keep up our momentum.

10% Braver means different things to different people as we smash down our internal glass ceiling, as we smash down the external glass ceiling, as we reach down and pull more women in education up the leadership ladder. As we nudge each other on, we have seen significant changes in the confidence of individuals in our community. Take one of our co-founders, Natalie Scott, as an example of being 10% Braver in action. Natalie resigned from a job that wasn't working for her and volunteered in the refugee camps in France. She started blogging about swapping her stilettos for wellies and about meeting a boy called Spider Man in The Jungle, which resulted in her winning *Tes* Blogger of the Year in 2016. Another #WomenEd member, realising that she was operating at a deputy headteacher level whilst called and paid as an assistant headteacher, re-negotiated her job title and salary. Two years later she started her first headship and nego-tiated flexibility as she has small children. These stories fill us with hope. These stories are why #WomenEd exists. We are not fixated on data, we are focused on people. We share our stories to enable others to grow and learn from them.

Finding and using our voices is at the heart of what we stand for and who we are. It is not simply about joining Twitter, but tweeting is a stepping stone to:

- writing a blog
- publishing an article
- speaking at a #LeadMeet
- running a workshop at a regional event
- contributing a key-note at our unconference
- writing a book

Over the last four years we have watched shy women starting their careers blossom in confi-dence. We have seen executive headteachers pay homage to the CEOs who have guided them on their journeys. We've listened to new mums, with their babies, share how they have drawn confidence from the community to apply for a promotion whilst on maternity leave.

Through such successes and wins, we are concerned by our collective reluctance to own and celebrate our accomplishments. Women seem to be more comfortable celebrating the achievements of each other than they are for their own success. Is this another gap we need to close? We are collectively challenging and slowly closing the confidence gap and the gender pay gap, so how can we close the 'I-got-a-promotion-and-I'm-proud-of-myself-but-I-don't-want-to-look-arrogant-by-publicly-sharing-it gap?'.

We encourage the #WomenEd community to share and celebrate each step they take on their leadership journeys. Our 10% Braver mantra has evolved into 10% Prouder and is developing into 10% Louder. The power of role models has been key to the success of #WomenEd and we encourage women leading in education to be brave and to do it, to be proud and to celebrate it, and to be loud and to share it to encourage and empower other women.

COLLABORATION

Setting up regional teams so that women could be connected and supported close to where they live and work means that #WomenEd has had significant impact for individuals and is affecting systemic change through its collaborative partnerships with various organisations. Here is a snapshot of some the work we have undertaken.

DEPARTMENT FOR EDUCATION (DfE)

We work closely with the DfE on their Women Leading in Education networks, their Coach-ing Pledge and their Diversity Grants. #WomenEd has a voice and has been invited to sit at the policy table. Our impact was mentioned in the DfE's White Paper 'Educational Excellence Everywhere', (DfE, 2016: 49) and, as a result, the DfE Women Leading in Education networks and the Women in Education's Coaching Pledge were launched. We are invited to contribute to the national agenda for flexible working, return to teaching, and female system leadership.

AMBITION SCHOOL LEADERSHIP

#WomenEd are working with Ambition School Leadership (formerly Teaching Leaders and Future Leaders) to pilot a National Professional Qualification for Headship for a women-only group. This space enables aspiring female headteachers to cover the content, secure the accreditation, consider personal and professional needs within the role, whilst networking with other female leaders and, importantly, to lead as women.

MATERNITY CPD

Emma Sheppard and the team of volunteers (@maternityCPD) created a network within #WomenEd for those on maternity leave to close the confidence and skills gap on returning to work. By challenging events that are not family friendly and providing professional learning opportunities whilst on maternity leave, we can keep women who might otherwise leave the profession to stay enfranchised.

MICROSOFT EDUCATION UK

We are grateful for the support of Microsoft Education UK since our first unconference. They hosted us for development days and national unconferences and worked with us to reduce the gender divide in technology, so strengthening the pipeline for more women to be digital leaders.

DAUNTLESS DAUGHTERS

Steph Green is one of our partners focused on changing things for the next generation of women by creating images that are 'brave, diverse, joyfilled and female' (Dauntless Daughters, n.d.). Challenging stereotypes and representing women who break the mould, our collaboration with this organisation aims to change the face of the future women leading in education.

#BAMEED, #LGBTED AND #DISABILITYED

These are our sister grassroots organisations who are hot on our heels. In our first three years of existence we became increasingly aware of the need for more diverse faces, voices, speakers and writers to be elevated by our community. We are champions of intersectionality for which we advocate together.

CHALLENGE

Intersectionality and unconscious bias are high on the #WomenEd agenda. Our events unveil the direct discrimination and unconscious bias that our community experiences in their roles, especially around progression, salary negotiation and returning to teaching after a career break.

The sad reality is that education may be a female-heavy sector, but leadership roles are not. The sad reality is that male leaders in the system are paid at a higher level than their female counterparts. The sad reality is that we see all white, all-male line ups ('manels') on national education stages with speakers from the same demographic. The sad reality is that women with families are forced to make the choice to leave the classroom because they do not want a full-time role or are forced to step down from leadership if they negotiate a flexible role. The sad reality is that, although we shine a spotlight on gender equality and diversity, more work needs to be done and we must look at the other protected characteristics. These are all issues with which this book is concerned.

Unconscious bias affects women leaders when applying for leadership roles, especially in science, technology, engineering and mathematics (STEM) areas. Stereotypical expectations around compliance, passivity, emotionality and resilience still exist and these are explored in Jules Daulby's chapter on gendered stereotypes. Wearing an engagement ring or having a baby bump affects our salary negotiation, which is explored further in Vivienne Porritt's chapter looking at the gender pay gap.

The glass ceiling for women in education is a reality. If we see shifts in the data for women progressing to headship, we are acutely aware that the national data hides the reality of system leadership. Data is not collated or reported on positions above the level of the named headteacher of a school, so in the case of academy headteachers, there is often an executive headteacher above them and a CEO above them. This means that, despite securing headship, the glass ceiling above some female leaders is silently being reinforced. At #WomenEd we all know and champion the women breaking through these glass ceilings, the women who are confidently and competently leading on data, timetabling, the curriculum, behaviour and digital learning. This is explored further in Claire Nicholls's chapter.

This situation is often worse for BAME (Black, Asian, Minority Ethnicities) women in education, and Sameena Choudry's chapter argues that, for these women, the glass ceiling has been replaced by one of concrete.

CHANGE

Across 2017 and the first half of 2018 we celebrated significant successes and impact. We launched:

- an app to keep everyone abreast of our events
- a newsletter (#WomenEd online) to share updates and links
- a blog to share reflections and help women to find their voices
- a digital leadership team (@WomenEd_Tech) to increase the number of women becoming digital leaders
- a book club (@WomenEdBookClub) as a half-termly opportunity to discuss topics in books by female authors or about women leadership, and Mary Beard joined us online for our first book discussion: *Women & Power*
- a pilot women-only National Professional Qualifications for Headship (NPQH) in partnership with Ambition School Leadership and Leading Women's Alliance

In Autumn 2017, we were shortlisted as an Outstanding Diversity Network in the National Diversity Awards, which helped us realise that our community was making a real difference. This was reiterated when we closed 2017 by being named in the *Tes's* inaugural Top Ten Education Influencers of 2017. We were delighted to be named and to find ourselves covered in the education press as far away as New Zealand as a result! We also joined other national stakeholders at a diversity roundtable chaired by Schools Minister Nick Gibb, to consult on the DfE's diversity agenda, and represented the voice of female teachers and leaders at a DfE summit on flexible working. This book, published with SAGE, enables us to share our story, mission and values beyond social media.

And yes, we did all of this alongside our day jobs. We cannot emphasise enough that our community are all volunteers. The generosity of the time and energy that members of the #WomenEd community share is humbling. The pay-it-forward mindset sees women sharing their expertise and experience to enable others to step up and lead.

#WomenEd challenges the characteristics of a modern leader as explored by Angela Browne in her chapter, which shows leaders and leadership can be different. A #WomenEd event in 2018 celebrated women who are breaking the mould by:

- embracing vulnerability
- using the resources they have
- concentrating
- opening their own school
- not knowing how to fit in
- fighting their fears
- choosing to be themselves
- doing what no-one expected them to do

Women educators who step up to lead should not be shoehorned into a man-sized mould, one they can't fill. Adapting Germaine Greer, we need to break the mould and create a female-shaped space in which we lead.

ROLE MODEL: KAREN GILES

Values-led leaders demonstrate that you can be a leader with a soul. Karen Giles is a primary headteacher in London and a facilitator for Ambition School Leadership. I remember meeting her at one of my first NPQH sessions where she invited 64 aspiring headteachers to go for a leisurely jog around the conference room. She was immaculately dressed in a purple shift dress, matching tailored jacket and heels and gracefully leapt like a gazelle. I fell a little bit in love with her on the spot.

I was delighted Karen came to my session on The Power of Networking at the second Leading Women's Alliance event. She is an old-school networker and I am a new one, and we had a passionate discussion about Shonda Rhimes' book *A Year of Yes*. We both agreed that whilst 'Yes' is an enabler, women also need to be empowered to say 'No!'.

Karen has local, regional, national and global impact as a leader. She has taught and led in London schools for 30 years. She recently completed a part-time secondment as a Local Authority School Effectiveness Lead Professional, working with leaders in 16 schools. Karen has been a leadership facilitator and coach for more than ten years, leading and facilitating a variety of mixed-phase coaching groups and workshops as well as working with both primary and secondary participants. She served as an Ofsted Inspector from 2010–15, and has been appointed as a coach and broker for the pan-London GLA Getting Ahead programme. She was the winner of the London Region National Teacher Award for Enterprise and Innovation in 2009 and serves as an advisory board member for the Varkey Foundation in the UK and Argentina. Karen currently serves as Headteacher, a position she has held for 15 years.

REFLECTIONS

- Why are you reading the #WomenEd book?
- How will it encourage you to be #10%braver?
- Can you identify, articulate and embody your core values as a person and a leader?
- What impact do you want this book to have on you personally and professionally?

REFERENCES

Berry, J. (2017) 'The lost leaders', reblogged on #WomenEd blog, May [Online]. Available at: https://womenedblog.wordpress.com/2017/10/05/lost-leaders/ (accessed 15 July 2018).

Dauntless Daughters (n.d.) Available at: http://dauntlessdaughters.co.uk/ (accessed 15 July 2018).

Department for Education (DfE) (2016) *Educational Excellence Everywhere*. London: DfE.

Future Leaders Trust (2015) *1700 Female Headteachers 'Missing' From England's Schools* [Press release]. Available at: www.future-leaders.org.uk/documents/62/1700_FEMALE_HEADS_MISSING_FROM_ENGLISH_SCHOOLS.pdf (accessed 16 July 2018).

Landsbaum, C. (2016) 'Obama's female staffers came up with a genius strategy to make sure their voices were heard', *The Cut*, 13 September [Online]. Available at: www.thecut.com/2016/09/heres-how-obamas-female-staffers-made-their-voices-heard.html (accessed 18 February 2018).

Marsh, H. (2017) 'What glass ceiling?', reblogged on #WomenEd blog, October [Online]. Available at: https://womenedblog.wordpress.com/2017/10/03/what-glass-ceiling-the-blog-birth-of-womened/ (accessed 15 July 2018).

Porritt, V. (2017) 'Connecting women leaders – the launch', reblogged on #WomenEd blog, October [Online]. Available at: https://womenedblog.wordpress.com/2017/10/13/connecting-women-leaders-the-launch/ (accessed 15 July 2018).

Rhimes, S. (2016) *A Year of Yes*. New York: Simon & Schuster.

Sandberg, S. (2013) *Lean In: Women, Work, and the Will to Lead*. New York: Knopf Doubleday Publishing Group.

2

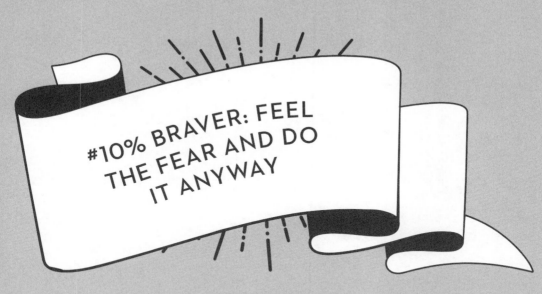

#10% BRAVER: FEEL THE FEAR AND DO IT ANYWAY

SUE COWLEY

KEY POINTS

This chapter will:

- Help you develop the confidence to be 10% braver and take the leaps you want to make in your career

- Explore your goals and how you can achieve them, while also helping you learn how to cope if you don't meet them

- Show you how to overcome 'imposter syndrome' and explain why you need to stop listening to your 'internal editor'

- Examine the power and importance of talking up your own achievements, and those of others

- Share an example of someone who inspired you to become 10% braver

INTRODUCTION

Once upon a time there was a girl who dreamed of being a professional dancer. From the age of 8, this was pretty much all that she wanted to do. (She also dreamed of being a writer, but she didn't see how anyone could make a living out of that, so she put that dream to one side for the time being.) Each day after school, the girl would go straight to dance classes at her local dance school. By the age of 12, she was taking classes and rehearsing for shows seven days a week. Her mum spent hours sewing beautiful tutus for her to wear in the shows. When she turned 16, the girl won a scholarship to go to a dance college, and when she got there she worked as hard as she could to realise her dream. She was lucky enough to be trained by amazing teachers, including Christopher Gable, who was a principal at the Royal Ballet and who starred in a movie called *The Boy Friend* (1971).

Then one day something terrible happened. Just as the girl was about to finish at dance college, and start to earn a living as a dancer, she got injured. Suddenly, her future was in tatters. The dream she had of being a dancer was over. The thing she had wanted to do for a decade was gone – vanished in a puff of smoke. She felt disorientated and confused, but she had no option but to pick herself up and start all over again.

A few years later, the girl was a fully grown woman. She had gone to college, learned to type, got herself a secretarial job, found a boyfriend and together they had bought a flat. When her boyfriend told her that she was really quite bright, and that she should go to university rather than be a secretary for the rest of her life (even though it would be difficult financially), she knew this was what she had to do. So it was that she followed in her mother's footsteps and became a teacher. A few more years later, the woman's partner came home one day and told her that his job was moving overseas. Would she go with him to see the world? Well, of course she would! And in the gap between leaving one teaching job in England and starting another in Portugal, she fulfilled her childhood dream of being a writer, by writing her first book.

Little did I know at the time, but I was living the #WomenEd values. I had found the confidence to seize new opportunities, and I was being (at least) 10% braver. So 20 years and 30 books later, I am lucky to be making a living from the thing I love to do. In this chapter I want to inspire you to take the leap into a role you have dreamed about. If your aspiration is to be a headteacher, or to take on a senior role in education or in another field, I want to help you find the confidence to take the leap, like I did 20 years ago. As my chapter title suggests, you will probably 'feel the fear', and your path may not be a smooth one, but think of what you might achieve if you dare!

I HAVE A DREAM

In the *Drawing the Future* report (Chambers et al., 2018), the authors asked young children from around the world to draw the kind of people they 'ideally want to become'. Even at the age of 7, the authors noted that 'children's aspirations appear to be shaped by gender-specific ideas about certain jobs' (2018: iv). Girls were more likely to choose caring roles; boys were more likely to choose practical roles, doing hands-on things. We need to analyse the kind of systemic factors that get in the way of our aspirations. One of the ways we can do this is to promote the values of #WomenEd to challenge stereotypes, and to provide new role models for young girls, particularly in our role as educators. As Ann Mroz, Editor of the *Tes* points out in *Drawing the Future*, 'it's hard to dream of being something you have never seen, or don't know even exists' (2018: xi). As well as an encouragement to 'dream big', children need to see people who model the things they dream about becoming.

The authors of the report noted how 'early on in their education, children already define career opportunities as male and female. When asked to draw a firefighter, a surgeon and a fighter pilot, 61 pictures were drawn of men and only 5 were female' (2018: 4). They found that 'men and women have different beliefs on their probability to succeed and will choose their career path according to these beliefs' (2018: 3). At an early age, confidence is already a key factor in career choices. This finding is supported by a study in the journal *Science*, where the authors found that '6- and 7-year old girls avoided participating in activities that were labelled for children who are "really, really smart"' (Bian et al., 2017: 389). The divide into gender roles starts early and it is vital that we challenge perceptions with our youngest learners. One way in which we can do this is by bringing women into our settings to talk about work in non-stereotypical careers. As leaders in education, we can effect change for the next generation of women, encouraging them to be brave and to take leaps into areas where there might be few females now.

WHAT'S THE WORST THAT CAN HAPPEN?

We are sometimes dismissive about encouraging children to 'follow their dreams'. Perhaps there is something in the British psyche that finds it distasteful for children (and perhaps particularly girls) to 'dream big'. Do we feel we are setting our children up for disappointment if we encourage them to reach for a goal that might be unattainable? Or is it better to let them believe that they can do anything, if they want to? If our goal is to encourage a growth mindset, as proposed by Carol Dweck (2006) in her book *Mindset*, we need to encourage them to aim high, and to be able to pick themselves up if they don't reach their goal. Even though I didn't fulfil my dream of being a professional dancer, the experiences that I had in pursuit of it have fed into everything I have done since, often in subtle ways. In a recent book, *The Artful Educator*, I talk about how teachers 'can take a number of lessons from the dancer' (Cowley, 2017: 171). The skills I developed when dancing – posture, non-verbal communication, movement – all feed into my teaching. They also feed into the way that I write, through the rhythm, movement and patterns inherent in language. None of our experiences are worthless, even if we don't fulfil the specific 'dream' we were aiming for.

Being 10% braver is about coming out of your comfort zone to take a small step, even though you find it scary. It is about acknowledging your dream and allowing yourself to believe that it is okay to prioritise it. Do you have a dream? I suspect you do, even if you have never admitted it to yourself. *If you could do anything, regardless of where it was, the skills or qualifications you needed or how much it paid, what would you do?* What is getting in the way of you taking small steps towards achieving that dream?

A great way to help yourself be more confident about taking the leap is to think about the worst thing that could happen if you try. It might sound strange to take a negative viewpoint like this. But what happens is that you realise your 'worst thing' doesn't sound that bad. When my partner was offered the job working overseas, we debated whether we should move abroad. In the end what decided it for us was the fact that we could move back home if it didn't work out. The job came to an end after a couple of years, and we moved back to the UK, but the experience was a brilliant one. Part of embarking on any adventure is the acceptance that it must come to an end.

THE CONFIDENCE GAP

In an article 'The Confidence Gap', authors Katty Kay and Claire Shipman (2014) describe their findings on confidence whilst researching their 2009 book *Womenomics*. Interviewing a range of successful women, Kay and Shipman made surprising discoveries about women's 'acute lack of confidence'. These women, in high profile positions, still express a lack of confidence about their achievements, a sense that they must have been 'just lucky'. Women who come across as confident may be judged more harshly, so women's perceived lack of confidence may also be socialised into them.

As a child I was shy, lacking in confidence, prone to extreme nervousness. While it might seem strange that someone who was nervous would dream about appearing on stage in front of hundreds of people, when you dance you take on a character. You become 'someone else', and through that character, and the language of dance, you express yourself without words. When it comes to lacking confidence, I have found that 'putting on a front' is a great help. Just as, when you are a teacher, you create a 'teacher character' to help you control and teach your class, so you can do the same thing in your dealings outside the classroom. Pretending to feel confident, even when you are not, can lead to you *feeling* more confident.

Not all kinds of confidence are the same. We tend to think of confident people as showy, brash, and happy to speak their minds. Ironically, though, some of the most outspoken people are a mess of insecurities underneath their confident exterior. Certainly some people are extroverts, and others present as introverts, as Susan Cain explores in her book *Quiet* (2013). But in between those two extremes is a continuum along which each of us can move, by taking deliberate steps to present ourselves as more confident. Becoming more confident does not mean you have to become an extrovert. Building your confidence can be about using a quiet inner strength to make your way through the world.

SILENCING THE CRITIC

A key issue for women can be concern about what other people will think about them. In 1978, psychologists Pauline Clance and Suzanne Imes coined the term 'Imposter Syndrome' – the feeling that, even when you are successful, you are just pretending to know what you are doing, that you are faking it. For writers, this problem asserts itself as something called the 'internal editor'. This is the voice that, as you write, whispers in your ear that what you have written is not good enough – that it is weird, or odd, or badly written, or that no one will like it. The internal editor causes writers to procrastinate, or to rewrite a piece repeatedly to try and make it 'work', before scrapping what they have written in disgust. A useful way to avoid this is to force yourself to aim for a word target – say 1,000 words – and not allow yourself to stop or edit until you have achieved it. Once you have something down on the page, your sense that you 'can do this' begins to build. In the same way, a new headteacher could list all their ideas for school improvement before focusing in on the ones they want to get in place first.

A bad review can hit a writer like a sucker punch. It is a similar effect to a teacher receiving bad feedback on a lesson observation, but magnified many times, because everyone in the public has access to your book. If you want to make a career in writing, you must get used to the idea that not everyone will like what you write. I explored this issue in a blog post entitled 'BAD review' (Cowley, 2014). If you are set on becoming a leader in education, you will face similar challenges. Sometimes you will have to make difficult decisions, and not everyone will agree with the decisions that you take. You must learn how to cope with criticism, in whatever form it takes, and bounce back from setbacks.

One key issue for female writers like myself to challenge is subconscious bias within publishing. The author Catherine Nichols decided to find out how deep this bias was, by sending out her novel under a male name. When she sent out her manuscript to agents with a male pseudonym, she was eight and a half times more likely to receive a query asking to see more. Even the rejection letters sent to 'George' were different from those sent to Catherine. The work was 'clever' and 'exciting' when 'George' had written it, whereas Catherine's female character had not been 'plucky' enough. Nichols describes how she was 'being conditioned like a lab animal against ambition' through the responses she received (Nichols, 2015). It's hard to fight against invisible discrimination, but there are ways. I kept seeing lists of recommended books by mainly male education authors shared on Twitter, so I collated and shared a list of female ones (Cowley, 2018). This is one way to try to live the #WomenEd values of connection, community and collaboration.

BECOMING 10% BRAVER

A few years ago, I was staying the night with my best friend in London. She is an amazing role model who runs a clinical trials unit for the NHS; a high-profile job done by an intelligent and confident woman. My friend said that she had been on a course where the presenter had asked the delegates: 'What would you do today if you were 10% braver?' I tucked the question away in my mind as I had a feeling it would come in handy at another time.

A year later, I used the question to inspire my keynote speech at the first #WomenEd unconference. I talked about leaps that I had made in my life, throwing in plenty of rude jokes and risqué props to get the audience laughing. I had planned to spend the last few minutes of my keynote reading out the song 'I Am Woman' by Helen Reddy. And then, as I got ready to read, the cry came from one of the founders of #WomenEd, Vivienne Porritt, to 'sing it, Sue! 10% braver!'. Of all the things that most terrify me, singing in public comes near the top of the list. But I could hardly refuse, having just talked about how everyone should be 10% braver. And so I found myself singing 'I am woman, hear me roar' in public, in front of a room of 200 relative strangers. And I promise you, if I can do that, you can do anything.

The great thing about being 10% braver is that it doesn't sound all that difficult. Perhaps this is why the mantra fits so perfectly with the #WomenEd values. It is not about being pushy, or shouting how great you are; it is just about trying something that makes you feel a bit nervous. It's being brave enough to take small steps towards an end goal, doing something that has always frightened you, or doing something to boost your self-image. Being 10% braver is not only about moving upwards in your career, but about taking life decisions, some of which might lead you in unexpected directions. In the time since that first speech, and since the #WomenEd network took on '10% braver' as a motto, I have seen countless women in the network use the mantra to push themselves in new ways. I have also been sent lots of direct messages from people asking me for advice on writing and telling me about the books they have written, inspired in part by the tagline. For example,

Rumbie Matambo (@RumbieMatambo) tweeted that she was 'Feeling #10%braver after attending my first #WomenEd event' (2018).

Portia Taylor (@MrsPTaylor) tweeted, 'After being 10% braver and very much inspired and supported by the amazing staff around me and the #WomenEd community, very proud to announce I am the acting deputy head for NHT-School come September' (2018).

Sameena Choudry (@EquitableEd) tweeted, '@Thelma_WalkerMP urging us to take risks and be brave, echoing our @WomenEd #10%braver mantra' (2018).

You can search Twitter for examples of how women (and men) have been braver. Put #10%braver and #WomenEd in the search bar and hundreds will come up, a wonderful source of inspiration.

BEHIND EVERY GREAT WOMAN

Of course, it's not as simple as thinking 'this is what I want to do' and doing it; there are other people involved in making it happen, and here the #WomenEd value of community comes into play. I would not have made a career as a writer and presenter if it were not for the support of my partner – from his insistence many years ago that I should do a degree, to his working while I spent time writing my first book, to his giving up his own career when mine took off, so that he could look after our children. Without his support I would not be where I am today.

A good support network is crucial if you are going to be able to take leaps and be 10% braver. The sources of support available to you will vary – it might be your family, your partner, your employer, your network of friends. From the female perspective, the support of men can be particularly important, because this is one way to show the next generation that men can take on what are thought of as traditionally female roles. The #HeForShe movement is a wonderful example of how men can be feminists as well.

IT'S NOT BOASTING

'It's not boasting if you can back it up.'

Muhammad Ali

Women can have a difficult relationship with their own achievements. While we might be able to acknowledge them to ourselves, the idea of talking about what we have achieved to others can feel a step too far. A colleague of mine called Laura Henry, who runs the #EYTalking community on Twitter, regularly reminds me of what Muhammad Ali says: that it is *not* boasting to share your achievements, if you can back them up. As a writer, I've had to come to terms with my discomfort around this issue. I don't like talking about my work but talking about my work is part of the job description. Marketing is an essential tool in the writer's toolkit. No one can read your book unless they know it exists.

One of the trickiest aspects of creating a book is the point at which you must write your own blurb for the back cover, saying what your book is about and why people should buy it. (I suspect many readers don't realise that authors write their blurbs themselves.) Because a blurb is written in the third person, it is a useful exercise in building your confidence about talking up your own achievements. By taking a step back from what you have achieved, it is somehow simpler to describe the things you have done in a positive light. As a leader in education, what would a blurb about *your* achievements say? As well as speaking out about our own achievements, we can also amplify those of other women in our networks, to help them build their careers and develop confidence in what they are doing. One way to do this is simply to retweet or email a message of support to a woman when you hear about something she has achieved.

IF IN DOUBT, JUST LEAP

'When in doubt, make a fool of yourself. There is a microscopically thin line between being brilliantly creative and acting like the most gigantic idiot on earth. So, what the hell, leap.'

Cynthia Heimel

This is one of my favourite quotes: it applies equally well to both teaching and writing – for me it sums up the creative process of being 10% braver and not caring what others think. When I'm working with teachers, I explain that it can be useful as an educator to be willing to make a fool of yourself, to not take yourself too seriously, to undermine the view of the teacher as an all-knowing 'authority', and to present yourself as someone willing to make mistakes and take creative risks. In this way, you present a model of a brave, creative person to your learners. The same applies to writing. You must go beyond what seems possible or sensible, to find something new and interesting. Sometimes these risks pay off and sometimes they don't, which is the nature of the creative process. If you spend your life worrying that someone else will think you foolish, you will find it harder to achieve your dreams.

ROLE MODEL: PINA BAUSCH

In the last year of my dance training, I went on a tour of Germany with a group of fellow students, to audition for various dance and ballet companies. One of the companies where we auditioned was Tanztheater Wuppertal Pina Bausch. Pina Bausch is a legend within the dance community, a woman who pushed at the boundaries of what was thought creatively possible or even sensible. Her work as a choreographer was as far from classical ballet as it was possible to get. It was even far away from what was accepted in contemporary dance at the time she started working. She created a controversial version of Stravinsky's *Rite of Spring* in 1975 and also worked with David Bowie during her life, which gives you an idea about how experimental she liked to be.

Bausch was a role model for me because she pushed at boundaries, and because she didn't appear to care what other people thought of her creative ideas. This is often an aspect of creativity. At first people think what you have done is shocking, or horrifying (think Tracey Emin's bed (1998) or Damien Hirst's shark (1991)), but once your work is accepted, people wonder why no one did it before. It takes courage to step out of the linear, and into the lateral, to do something unexpected or surprising. For me, the chance to audition for Pina Bausch was a highlight of my dancing days.

10% BRAVER: FEEL THE FEAR AND DO IT ANYWAY IN ORGANISATIONS

As a prospective leader in education, or as someone who already has a leadership role in a school, you will want to support and encourage your staff to feel like valued members of your team and to take creative risks. But for them to do this, you need to give them permission to fail. In a climate where educators are under pressure, and where the accountability regime has pretty much everyone on edge, this can be difficult to do. You will need to take the chance that some of your staff may struggle to achieve what you need them to do. They must step outside their comfort zones and accept the possibility that what they try might not work. This can create considerable pressures for you as the person in authority. It is very tempting to take on more of the work yourself, rather than delegate and run the risk that others will not be as efficient or competent as you might be. You need to be there for your staff, to help them pick themselves up ready to try again if things don't go right. Handing over trust requires us to be brave, so apply the 10% braver mantra to the way that you lead your team.

Here are three 10% braver challenges that you might like to get your staff to try:

- Team teach with a friend, outside the subject or age group you normally teach
- Organise an event for the students or for the local community, something you've never done before
- Do a job swap for a day with someone else in the organisation

CHANGING THE SYSTEM FROM WITHIN

If we're going to change the system, we must keep asking ourselves difficult questions. We need to keep facing our challenges head on, working together within our networks to challenge stereotypes and to build progress through collaboration. I'd like to finish this chapter with five questions to get you thinking about how you might do this, and where you might want to go next:

- What are the main factors that stop you from taking the leaps you would like to in your career?
- What sources of support do you have, or can you find, to help you develop and take leaps?
- In what ways can you act as a source of support for others?
- Do you feel that it is boastful to talk about your accomplishments? How can you share your successes without feeling embarrassed about it?
- How do you cope with failure, and how could you get better at dealing with it?

And of course, it is only right that I finish with the question that inspired the now famous #WomenEd tag line . . .

What would you do today if you were 10% braver?

REFERENCES

Bian, L., Leslie, S-J. and Cimpian, A. (2017) 'Gender stereotypes about intellectual ability emerge early and influence children's interests', *Science*, *355* (6323): 389–391.

Cain, S. (2013) *Quiet: The Power of Introverts in a World that Can't Stop Talking*. London: Penguin Books.

Chambers, N. Kashefpakdel, Dr E.T., Rehill, J. and Percy, C. (2018) *Drawing the Future*, Education and Employers Research Report. Available at: www.educationandemployers.org/wp-content/uploads/2018/01/DrawingTheFuture.pdf (accessed 15 July 2018).

Choudry, S. [@Equitable Ed] (2018) 17 March [Twitter]. Available at: https://twitter.com/EquitableEd/status/974977867930066944 9 (accessed 18 July 2018).

Cowley, S. (2014) 'BAD Review' [blog]. Available at: https://suecowley.wordpress.com/2014/11/09/bad-review/ (accessed 18 July 2018).

Cowley, S. (2017) *The Artful Educator*. Carmarthen: Crownhouse Publishing.

Cowley, S. (2018) *100 Female Education Authors*. Available at: www.suecowley.co.uk/100-female-education-authors.html (accessed 18 July 2018).

Dweck, C. (2006) *Mindset: How You Can Fulfil Your Potential*. New York: Ballatine Books.

Emin, T. (1998) *My Bed* [Installation Artwork]. London: Tate Gallery.

Hirst, D. (1991) *The Physical Impossibility of Death in the Mind of Someone Living* [Installation Artwork]. London: Saatchi Gallery.

Kay, K. and Shipman, C. (2009) *Womenomics*. New York: HarperBusiness.

Kay, K. and Shipman, C. (2014) 'The confidence gap', *The Atlantic*, May [Online]. Available at: www.theatlantic.com/magazine/archive/2014/05/the-confidence-gap/359815/ (accessed 15 July 2018).

Matambo, R. [@RumbieMatambo] (2018) 9 June [Twitter]. Available at: https://twitter.com/RumbieMatambo/status/1005485133653336064 (accessed 18 July 2018).

Nichols, C. (2015) 'Homme de Plume: What I learned sending my novel out under a male name', *Jezebel*, April [Online]. Available at: https://jezebel.com/homme-de-plume-what-i-learned-sending-my-novel-out-und-1720637627 (accessed 15 July 2018).

Taylor, P. [@MrsPTaylor] (2018) 4 May [Twitter]. Available at: https://twitter.com/MrsPTaylor/status/992476441156694016 (accessed 18 July 2018).

3

PINK AND BLUE LIMIT US ALL

JULES DAULBY

KEY POINTS

This chapter will:

- Ask why everything is gendered, even cheese?

- Highlight the need to be aware of inherent bias

- Explore raising and teaching our children in a gender balanced world

- Share implications for women leading in education

INTRODUCTION

I was asked to join #WomenEd by Vivienne Porritt because of my interest in gender balance. A growing industry of pink for girls and women and blue for boys and men frustrated me so much that I created a hashtag called #genderedcheese [Twitter, online]. There are so many visual and gendered messages telling us who should lead and who should look pretty. I was increasingly angry with the images I saw on social media, especially with a teacher training advert promoting leadership opportunities using three young white males. Then I saw a picture of two cheeses that were identical, except the yellow one was marketed to girls and the blue one targeted boys. Eureka – #genderedcheese was born and is a lens through which the #WomenEd community views messages to and about women.

I have given a #genderedcheese presentation each year since our first unconference. In 2015, I shocked the audience with images of a pink babygro emblazoned with 'I hate my thighs' and a blue one with 'superhero' across the front. I also showed two adverts about litter, with a good-looking male saying 'Pick it up, it's the clever thing to do' and a sexy female saying 'Pick it up, it's the pretty thing to do'. There were plenty more images, including male-only conference panels and pink and blue Kinder Eggs interspersed with more serious inequalities in leadership representation. In 2017 I showed an image of a girl (taken from the arts education organisation Curved House Kids) with science, technology, engineering and mathematics (STEM) facts around her. Table 3.1 shows equitable take up of these subjects at 14 years old, inequality widening at 16 years old and a very low take up of STEM subjects by young women in higher education.

Table 3.1 Take up of STEM subjects

	14 years old for GCSE	16 years old forA level	Higher education
Female	50%	35%	9%
Male	50%	65%	29%

(Based on WISE, 2017)

Matched the data from Table 3.1 with an image of the House of Commons' Science and Technology Committee, which would discuss how to increase the number of women in STEM careers, and which, in September 2017, was made up of eight men and no women (Asthana, 2017)! By 2017 the committee comprised three women and seven men which is only a slight improvement (Commons Select Committee: Science and Technology, 2017).

#genderedcheese also gives me the opportunity to highlight #manels (all male panels) and yes, in education where over 80% of the workforce are female, there are still #manels. It happens less now, except ironically, at #WomenEd events when we plan #HeForShe panels. #HeForShe is a hashtag that welcomes men to our network because solutions are in the hands of both genders; we must encourage men to join us as much as women. There are some great word associations for #genderedcheese: cheese boards, big cheeses, cheesed off, cheesy – all deliberately used alongside the hashtag. This chapter will help you explore the concept of gender balance and, if you're in the dark and confused by hashtags and social media, it will also give you links to delve deeper into the world of #genderedcheese.

WHAT DOES BEING GENDERED MEAN?

If something is gendered, we attribute certain characteristics to it that are not biological, for example assuming women are fragile or imagining the man in the room is in charge. We perceive and treat men and women differently due to societal attitudes rather than physiological differences. Implicit and explicit stereotypes are everywhere, in language, marketing, the media and, most importantly for #WomenEd, in decision-making positions. The drip, drip of pink and blue means gendered language is pervasive, such as David Cameron asking a fellow Member of Parliament to 'calm down dear', or, as a recent study noted, women being attributed with compassion and men seen as analytical (Smith et al., 2018a). The journalist Arwa Mahdawi says, 'language reflects and reinforces social norms and ungendering language is an important part of solving sexism' (2017). Language pervades our society to the point we don't even notice. Consider 'man up', 'grow a pair' or 'you throw like a girl' – these phrases assume that men must be brave and women are weak. @beingmankind (https://twitter.com/beingmankind) produced a book challenging stereotypes such as 'boys don't cry' and the damaging connotations of 'grow a pair'. #genderedcheese highlights gendered language and images often used in children's toys, a topic also explored by @lettoysbetoys (https://twitter.com/LetToysBeToys). Casual sexism is highlighted brilliantly by @everydaysexism (https://twitter.com/EverydaySexism).

Draw-a-Scientist is an open-ended experiment that has run since 1966, asking over 20,000 children to draw what a scientist looks like. Most children draw males, but over the years the percentage of female scientists represented has increased from fewer than 1% in 1966 to 36% in 2016 (Gray, 2018). Importantly however, as children get older they are more likely to draw male scientists, suggesting stereotyping becomes more pervasive as children get older. Is it any wonder when shop aisles are full of pink for girls and blue for boys, princesses for girls and scientist images for boys? These subliminal messages go deep, as shown in the BBC2 TV programme *No More Boys and Girls: Can Our Kids Go Gender Free?* (Abdelmoneim, 2017), which also described how gendered attitudes are fixed by the age of 6. Another study in the US, by Bian et al. (2017), found that by 5 years old, girls were likely to ascribe 'brilliance' to their own gender but at 6 and 7 they gave boys this attribute. A total of 65% of boys assigned their own gender to 'really, really smart', whereas girls did only 48% of the time (Bian et al., 2017: 389). These findings sadden and worry me.

Fairy tales and children's literature are steeped in gender stereotyping and are likely to influence a child's early perception of gender. They present the archetypal motifs of women as nasty and old or young and pretty, waiting to be saved to live happily ever after. Archetypes are 'primitive mental images from the earliest human ancestors' and in Jungian theory, are present in the 'collectively inherited unconscious' (Oxford Reference, 2018). The word archetype derives from the Greek adjective 'first-moulded', and such ancient stereotypes pervade society today: women being saved by men, women's value attached to how beautiful they are, and old women being witches or evil, ugly sisters. Thinking critically about fairy tales (not banning them, I'd add!) has been introduced in Victoria, Australia as part of a 'Respectful Relationships' curriculum (Victoria State Government, n.d.). Their intention is to promote gender equality and the curriculum begins in the early years with fairy tales. This includes examining Disney's more modern versions of fairy tales, such as *Frozen* and *Tangled*, which present female characters more fully and perhaps less helpless. Julia Donaldson is one of many children's authors who attempt to turn stories and gender stereotypes on their head. My favourite is *Zog* (Donaldson, 2010). The tale begins in knight school with boys being taught how to slay dragons and save princesses. However, the princess didn't want to be rescued or be a princess and the story ends with the dragon, Zog, becoming the flying doctor for the princess, and the knight, her nurse.

Campaigning for gender equality is not just for the empowerment of women however; social influence affects both sexes. Breaking preconceived ideas of certain roles and characteristics for both genders is vital for a gender-neutral society where balance and choice are available. This is where #genderedcheese, while light-hearted, has a serious message. It is the explicit and implicit messages we send out and the preconceptions we have within us which make the biggest difference. This includes a girl thinking she can't wear a superhero costume because she must be a princess, and the board of a multi-academy trust made up *entirely of white men*. Sue Cowley queries 'why no one in this MAT stopped to think that this might be a problem' (2017). We ask this question regularly. An attempt to make decision-makers as diverse as possible, reflecting the communities they serve, will, in some part, negate the internal biases we all hold. Did you know that female lecturers in universities get less positive feedback than their male peers (Bates, 2015)? Did you know that an orchestra recruiting new members found that, once applications were made blind, they hired more women and British Asian and Minority Ethnic (BAME) musicians than previously (Rice, 2013)? Hearing only the professional voice of the musicians helped, but the screens didn't make as much impact as recruiters wanted: 'the telltale signs of women's shoes' could still affect implicit bias so candidates were asked to remove their shoes before blind auditions! No matter how inclusive we think we are, all data and research point us to the fact that we are influenced by our unconscious bias. Penny Rabiger is a co-founder of #BAMEed, a group which, inspired by #WomenEd, created a similar network to highlight the even more dire representation of the BAME community in education. In conversation with Penny, she went further than influence, saying 'unconscious makes it seem as if we aren't responsible. Inherent suggests what it is; deeply engrained and conditioned into us by society'.

There are times when I am challenged about #genderedcheese and told labels don't explicitly say boys and girls even when products are coloured in pink and blue. This suggests a lack of understanding of the subliminal messages that children, as young as 3, understand. Enough people stereotype things for marketing departments and their lazy branding to flourish. A recent example I used at the #WomenEd 2017 Unconference was a photograph of two girls' shirts, one with a princess on the front and the phrase 'always ready to smile', the other with 'hey cutie' in a speech bubble. As part of my disruption, I asked our community to swap clothes around, showing them how a green top with 'future scientist' from the boys' section looked hung between the two girls' tops. When faced with such an image it seems obvious that we should have gender-balanced clothes. Some supermarkets are attempting to become more gender-balanced in their clothes and products, but we are still a long way off. Images may not explicitly say boys and girls, but society understands the code. It is, as Jung describes, in our 'collective unconscious'. Even when Star Wars included a female protagonist, a model of Rey was invisible in toy departments, causing an outcry that toy companies did not produce the same range of toys as with previous film heroes (Rivera, 2016). Gender stereotypes leave both girls and boys with little choice. If we continue to tell boys that they will be astronauts and girls that they will be carers, we are signalling their aspirations and their worth, and may be limiting what each gender can become.

YOU CAN'T BE WHAT YOU CAN'T SEE

Let's explore how gender stereotyping looks in practice. Anton Jones and Eliana Anand were born in 2018. How will their lives map out?

It starts in the baby unit in hospital. Anton wears a little blue hat, tucked in with a blue blanket and sporting a blue babygro with 'Superman' emblazoned across his chest. Eliana on the other hand courts a pink hat, a pink blanket and a pink babygro with 'I hate my thighs' written across it. Whilst most would recognise a stock phrase that is supposed to be funny, the future for Eliana begins here. Those who dress her will tell her to look pretty and to use plenty of remedies to improve as she grows up, from smoothing out her skin with an anti-cellulite cream and losing weight with a slimming group to plastic surgery, to look like the photoshopped images of celebrities seen in magazines and on social media. In contrast, Anton needs to rescue people, be strong and display out-of-the-ordinary characteristics; Anton will protect and save the world. If he can't do sport, he may be told he throws like a girl, and when he cries, rather than being consoled, Anton will be told that boys don't cry. The books Eliana receives contain princesses who need to be rescued; Anton is given tales of boisterous boys taking risks. As they grow up, Eliana will be cooking on her toy kitchen and pretending to hoover, 'like mummy' preparing the home. Anton will be building this home from Lego, when he's not discovering space on his rocket, that is. By age 6, these stereotypes will be fixed.

Once Eliana and Anton are at school full time, our children's learning is passed to their peers, teachers and media influence; the wider world now has impact. Children have been influenced by the toys they played with and building Lego will have improved Anton's mathematical skills and spatial awareness, whereas cognitive sequencing and early language skills have been embedded for Eliana in caring for the home in many guises of merchandising (Oksman, 2016). Ros Ball and James Millar's The Gender Agenda (2017) is a brilliant example of how children lead gendered lives. As parents, they were surprised at how pervasive gender culture is and how family members, teachers, the media, toys, films and merchandising influenced, at best, and controlled, at worst, what their children should wear, behave and think. I was once told off by someone in the supermarket as my son had a pink dummy in his mouth. Such policing, when people are cross with you for not adhering to their gendered perceptions, can be damaging. In a tweet, Michael Conroy (2018), founder of the Men At Work Organisation, describes gendered language as 'a complex and reflexive web of policing according to internalised yardsticks'.

Anton and Eliana are now 7 and many ideas are fixed. Anton receives a skateboard for his birthday; the skate park is full of boys skating with girls chatting and watching. Eliana sees this as she walks past with her mum to go to her dance class. She is dressed in her princess outfit and wears a t-shirt with 'Smile and be pretty' on the front. Anton is trying out lots of tricks on his new scooter, confident to fail and happy to take risks despite having hurt himself a few times. He won't cry when he hurts himself though; last time he did that he was told to 'man up' by his dad. Both Eliana and Anton are learning to mask instincts and feelings – Anton as the brave knight and Eliana as the compliant princess.

Are we raising our girls to be perfect and raising our boys to be brave? In a TED Talk (2016), Reshma Saujani, the founder of Girls Who Code, suggests that women's desire for perfection makes them overly cautious. In the US, 600,000 jobs are available in computing and technology; and for the American population to grow and truly innovate, we cannot leave women behind, says Saujani, as well as saying that we should socialise girls to be comfortable with imperfection and value courage instead. This is one of the reasons why Microsoft Education UK collaborated with #WomenEd to reduce the gender divide in technology.

At 16, Anton and Eliana are making subject choices for A levels. Anton has chosen the sciences and maths, and Eliana, despite getting excellent grades in her GCSEs, has opted for languages and the arts. Eliana thinks the boys in her class are cleverer than her and has learned to keep quiet in discussions, letting others take the lead for fear of being called bossy again. Her teachers praised her efforts at parents' evening, calling her compassionate, but warned against her becoming emotional. Anton was described as analytical, but teachers warned he could come across as arrogant. The University of Oxford suggests that 'sixth-form students are already internalising gender stereotypes when it comes to their career choices' (University of Oxford Careers Service, 2015).

What are Eliana and Anton's ambitions? Let us imagine that they grow up and both have teaching careers. Eliana has seen a job for assistant headteacher. She works part time and doesn't feel as noticed or as valued due to her career break. Childcare is also costing a fortune. Whilst deep down she thinks she could do the job, systemic difficulties put up too many barriers for her to do a job that will fit with her family and home life. She describes herself as 'just part-time', and a member of staff recently called her 'a hobby teacher'. As she puts out the washing, Eliana can feel the stereotypes she learned as a child repeating.

Anton is still in the science board meeting at school and regularly misses his children's bedtimes. He is ambitious and was pleased when he listed his many achievements as Head of Science to his boss, which put him in a good position when he applied for the assistant headteacher role. He negotiated a better salary, knowing this was more than the other two female assistant heads. There was an implicit understanding, when he asked for more money, that he had a family to support as the primary provider. Anton stays late after work and often bumps into his headteacher, who happened to tell him that one of the deputy heads was leaving and the role would be advertised soon. He knew he would apply despite lacking several of the specifications required for the role. He rings home to tell his wife he will be late as it would be good to begin preparing his application. As the school is becoming a multi-academy trust (MAT), Anton knew that, one day, he would become a chief executive of a MAT. He was prepared to move anywhere in the country for promotions to reach his ambitions.

IMPLICATIONS FOR WOMEN LEADING IN EDUCATION

Often, careers are based upon being visible in the workplace after hours rather than on the results achieved. Education Datalab's research suggested that, at senior leader positions, women were more likely to be promoted internally and less likely to move locations for their careers (2015). Careers for women can be affected by out-of-hours work, childcare limitations or quite simply just having children. But how are they judged? What are the attributes women are praised for and does this differ from men? A study by Smith et al. (2018a) explored language linked to performance indicators in the military; they analysed 4,000 participants and 81,000 evaluations looking at objective and subjective measures. There were no differences in objective measures, for example fitness and grades, but when looking at subjective evaluations, although men and women received an equal number of positive attributes (in which men were most frequently praised for being 'analytical', 'competent' and 'athletic' and women for being 'compassionate', 'enthusiastic' and 'energetic'), women were assigned significantly more negative ones. Negative attributes used frequently to describe women's performance included 'inept', 'selfish', 'frivolous', 'passive', 'scattered', 'gossip'. This research suggests a double bind whereby women who are perceived as communal or compassionate are seen as lacking in competence, whereas those seen as more competent are perceived as cold and uncaring (Smith et al., 2018b: 3).

A common response when we discuss marginalised groups, such as women in leadership positions, is an argument that it should be the best person (some still use the word 'man') for the job. This premise suggests that if organisations proactively seek out women or use quotas, the field will be substandard. This is despite boards of directors in the UK being only 22% female (Turner, 2017), only 32% of Members of Parliament in the UK being women (Keen and Cracknell, 2018) and in education there being a disproportionately higher representation of men in leadership positions. This may be why job adverts for leadership posts still use gendered language, which can result in fewer female applications, especially in the secondary sector. According to Vivienne

Porritt, 'It's just not how [women] see themselves or how they want to do leadership when they get there' (quoted in Tickle, 2018). Until society encourages women to be in decision-making positions, we are missing out on some of our best leaders in education.

The reasons for underrepresentation of women in senior positions and the overrepresentation of women in low-paid jobs such as in the care sector are complex, but, we argue, much is because 'you can't be what you can't see'. Structural systems seem to be stuck in a post-war scenario where men are the primary earners, supported by a stay-at-home or work-part-time-whether-you-choose-to-or-not wife. How these structural systems and mindsets affect the world of work is shown in two McKinsey reports, *Making the Breakthrough* (2012) and *Unlocking the Full Potential of Women at Work* (2012) (Barsh, 2012). Men were more likely to be promoted based on perceived potential, yet women were promoted on the basis of their performance.

When presenting at a #WomenEd event entitled Difficult Women, Dr Maja Korica, from the University of Warwick, told us how appearance is an obvious difference in leadership, citing an article comparing the corporate world to gorilla society, 'where power belongs to silverback males'. Korica says that although provocative, there are worryingly accurate similarities. 'Bosses spread themselves out behind their large desks. They stand tall when talking to subordinates. Their conversation is laden with prestige pauses and declarative statements' (Schumpeter, 2014). What is needed instead lies at the heart of #WomenEd: 'purposefully and openly recognising that while difference can seem and be difficult, its desirability trumps both tradition, and our personal ease' (Korica, 2018).

AGITATE FOR CHANGE

With clarity and conviction, we can change. To eradicate #genderedcheese we must be proactive in our own behaviour and ensure that decision-makers make bold changes to redress the balance. To begin:

- Go to a #WomenEd event, join our community on Twitter (@WomenEd), search through #genderedcheese
- Commit to no more #manels (male-only panels)
- Find more female chairs of governors and trustees and stop the #genderedcheese boards
- Be proactive in ensuring diverse representation at all levels and especially in leadership; put yourself forward for opportunities and posts

ORGANISATIONAL PERSPECTIVES

In exploring how to create a healthy gender balance within schools and our own lives as teachers, what could make Eliana and Anton's lives more balanced? Eliana can make some changes herself. The starting point for these are some searching, personal questions: What are my ambitions? What choices do I want to make? How can I boost my confidence?

How can Anton change? We don't want to quash his ambitions, but to enact change he needs to be proactive in his approach to equality, for example by fighting for transparency in salaries, modelling good practice and perhaps volunteering to coach women to leadership positions. He can boost the numbers of girls choosing STEM subjects as Tim Ennion has demonstrated

(Ennion, 2018). As he gets promoted, Anton can recognise his privileged position and ensure that, when he becomes the CEO of a MAT, he listens and takes on #WomenEd's recommendations: blind applications, removing the request for current salaries in applications, adopting flexible working, and hiring a genius timetabler to ensure he can keep and promote the best person for the job, knowing that as many barriers for women have been removed as possible. This would make Anton a fully fledged #HeForShe!

Governors and senior leaders can lead and foster a culture that is gender neutral, ethical and equitable. To do so requires a value-driven approach to all aspects of a school, but for the purposes of this section we will look more closely at creative and equitable solutions leaders can use to attract and retain experienced staff.

- On a basic level, leaders must directly engage with the clarity of these issues, recognise that they exist and raise awareness of the positive effects a more equitable and gender-neutral working environment can bring for all staff.
- The equitable ethos of a school must be communicated through job adverts, for example by targeting returning teachers and by highlighting what a school offers in terms of flexible practice, job shares and part-time opportunities for leaders.
- Give messages that all are welcome; schools need talent rather than convenient structures.
- Consider blind recruitment applications where personal identifiers are removed from applications.
- Avoid recruitment decisions that favour an employee whose life is compatible with traditional school systems over a superior candidate who has complexities outside of work.
- Never hire, pay more or promote simply because your unconscious bias tells you that a man must feed his family!
- Remove the request that applicants list their current salary on applications as this reduces negotiating power.
- Offer senior leadership positions on both a part-time and full-time basis.
- Normalise parental leave and have leaders model this behaviour through their own actions. Male leaders, especially, should encourage men to take paternity leave to establish this as a more frequent, unremarkable choice for male teachers to take.
- Consider the possibility of an onsite crèche or nursery to support staff with very young children.

CHANGING THE SYSTEM

A more gender-balanced culture cannot be created by schools and education organisations alone; much of this needs to happen in the home. As such, here are some top tips for parents on fostering a culture that is gender neutral, ethical and equitable:

- Ensure your son, as well as your daughter, reads books that feature influential women, such as Kate Pankhurst's *Fantastically Great Women Who Changed the World* (2016).
- Ensure that parental advice is not clouded by gender stereotypes that can disempower and perpetuate harmful behaviours. Consider, for example, this from the male charity Mankind: 'Don't tell your daughters not to go out at night, tell your sons to behave.'

- Rearrange supermarket shelving to become gender balanced; let people choose for themselves, especially children.
- Encourage careers not driven by stereotypes, so that, for example, opportunities for future careers in science are targeted at both genders.

Most significantly, recognise that equality and equity aren't the same thing: as Shanna Peeples, winner of the 2015 National Teacher Award, said, 'Equality is everyone gets shoes. Equity is that all the shoes fit' (Graeper, 2016).

QUESTIONS

- Are there aspects of gender stereotyping, either overt or more implicit, that prevent a more equitable culture in your school or organisation from flourishing?
- Does the leadership within your school, or educational organisation, directly engage with these issues? Are there ways in which you can proactively encourage awareness, debate and action?
- Look at the media messages, commercial imagery and language that you come across as part of daily life. Can you find examples of #genderedcheese that need to be called out?

ROLE MODELS: JULIA GILLARD AND NICOLA STURGEON

If you want to change the society, educate a girl

Julia Gillard

Are politicians the new princesses? Many of us have female politicians as role models as we see them in positions that can make a difference. We see how powerful they can be but also how vilified they often become. Irrespective of political sides, many morph into witches like Theresa May, Margaret Thatcher and Julia Gillard, Australia's previous prime minister, where in Australia 'burn the witch' was repeatedly chanted before she lost her premiership.

I have huge admiration for these women, and I have chosen two political leaders as my role models. I still get goose bumps when I watch Julia Gillard's response, in October 2012, to the then opposition leader, Tony Abbott, on misogyny (Gillard, 2012). If you haven't seen it, it is still one of the most powerful feminist responses to sexism I've seen. Gillard has recently established the Global Institute for Women's Leadership at King's College London, where she acts as chair, and seeks to 'bring together rigorous research, practice and advocacy to better understand and address the causes of women's under-representation in leadership positions across sectors and countries and the way gender negatively impacts the evaluation of women leaders' (Kings College London, 2018).

My second role model is Nicola Sturgeon. She is a powerful leader and created a Scottish Cabinet with a 50:50 gender balance (Brooks, 2014). Her speech for An Lantair to mark International Women's Day in 2017 is a paean to women's leadership:

> I got quite a lot of letters and e-mails asking me how I could be sure that all the women in the Cabinet were there on merit.
>
> I didn't get a single letter asking whether all of the men were there on merit. ... I believe that people should succeed based on how good they are and how hard they work but if we had a genuine meritocracy in our country right now then women, who represent more than 50% of the population, would already be equally represented. (Sturgeon, 2017)

I hope that current female politicians will not be airbrushed from history as Mo Mowlam was in the media coverage of the twentieth anniversary of The Good Friday Agreement (Williams, 2018). When Nicola Sturgeon responded to being labelled as a 'dangerous woman' alongside other female leaders she responded:

> Terms like 'dangerous' can belittle the positions of women in power by implying that we should be feared, and I am extremely concerned that women can be collectively branded in a way that men are simply not subjected to. Despite this I took great pride in being termed 'dangerous' when I considered those with whom I shared the title, such as Liberty director Shami Chakrabarti and German Chancellor Angela Merkel. (Dangerous Women Project.org, 2016)

As with Theresa May being called a 'bloody difficult woman', it seems that being a female leader can bring with it undeserved titles purely for having ambition. This, like #genderedcheese, is the princess fighting back and wanting to save herself rather than be saved.

REFERENCES

Abdelmoneim, J. (2017) *No More Boys and Girls: Can Our Kids Go Gender Free?* BBC2 [Online]. Available at: www.bbc.co.uk/programmes/b09202jz (accessed 14 July 2018).

Asthana, A. (2017) 'Commons science committee needs women, says Norman Lamb' *The Guardian* 13 September [Online]. Available at: https://www.theguardian.com/politics/2017/sep/13/commons-science-committee-needs-a-woman-says-norman-lamb (accessed 27 December 2018).

Ball, R. and Millar, J. (2017) *The Gender Agenda*. London: Jessica Kingsley Publishers.

Barsh, J. and Yee, L. (2012) 'Unlocking the full potential of women at work', McKinsey & Company [Online]. Available at: https://www.mckinsey.com/~/media/McKinsey/Business%20Functions/Organization/Our%20Insights/Unlocking%20the%20full%20potential%20of%20women%20at%20work/Unlocking%20the%20full%20potential%20of%20women%20at%20work.ashx (accessed 4 December 2018).

Bates, L. (2015) 'Female academics face huge sexist bias – no wonder there are so few of them', *The Guardian*, 13 February [Online]. Available at: www.theguardian.com/lifeandstyle/womens-blog/2015/feb/13/female-academics-huge-sexist-bias-students (accessed 14 July 2018).

Bian, L., Leslie, S.J. and Cimpian, A. (2017) 'Gender stereotypes about intellectual ability emerge early and influence children's interests', *Science*, *355*(6323): 389–391.

Brooks, L. (2014) 'Nicola Sturgeon announces Scottish cabinet with equal gender balance', *The Guardian*, 21 November [Online]. Available at: www.theguardian.com/politics/2014/nov/21/nicola-sturgeon-scottish-cabinet-equal-gender-balance (accessed 14 July 2018).

Commons Select Committee: Science and Technology (2017) *Membership*. Available at: www.parliament.uk/business/committees/committees-a-z/commons-select/science-and-technology-committee/membership/ (accessed 14 July 2018).

Conroy, M. [@MichaelConroy68] (2018) 'Yes, it's a complex and reflexive web of policing according to internalised yardsticks of what is appropriate', 11 July [Tweet]. Available at: https://twitter.com/michael-conroy68/status/1016947497023963137 (accessed 14 July 2018).

Cowley, S. (2017) 'Represent', *Freeing the Angel*, December [Online]. Available at: https://suecowley.word press.com/2017/12/12/represent/ (accessed 14 July 2018).

Dangerous Women Project.org (2016) *Scottish First Minister Nicola Sturgeon explains what being labelled a 'dangerous woman' means for her*, 22 March. Available at: http://dangerouswomenproject.org/2016/03/22/dangerous-women-change-world/ (accessed 14 July 2018).

Donaldson, J. (2010) *Zog*. London: Alison Green Books/Scholastic.

Education Datalab (2015) 'Women dominate the teaching profession, but men are winning the pay game', in *Seven Things You Might Not Know About Our Schools* (pp. 24–26) [Online]. Available at: https://ffteduca tiondatalab.org.uk/wp-content/uploads/2016/02/EduDataLab-7things.pdf (accessed 14 July 2018).

Ellingrud, K., Krishnan, M. and Madgavkar, A. (2016) *Miles to Go: Stepping up Progress Toward Gender Equality*, McKinsey Global Institute, September [Online]. Available at: www.mckinsey.com/featured-in sights/gender-equality/miles-to-go-stepping-up-progress-toward-gender-equality (accessed 14 July 2018).

Ennion, T. (2018) *Teachers' Moral Purpose Will Get Us Through*, #WomenEd Blog, January [Online]. Available at: https://womenedblog.wordpress.com/2018/01/18/teachers-moral-purpose-will-get-us-through/ (accessed 15 July 2018).

Gillard, J. (2012) *Julia Gillard's Misogyny Speech*, YouTube, October [Online]. Available at www.youtube.com/watch?v=SOPsxpMzYw4 (accessed 14 July 2018).

Graeper, J. (2016) '2016 National Advisory Council: Equity in Education', *Scolastic Edu*, May [Online]. Available at: http://edublog.scholastic.com/post/2016-national-advisory-council-equity-education (accessed 14 July 2018).

Gray, A. (2018) *Kids Aren't Biased At Age 6. And Then This Happens*, World Economic Forum, May [Online]. Available at: www.weforum.org/agenda/2018/03/kids-aren't-biased-at-6-and-then-this-happens/ (accessed 14 July 2018).

Keen, R. and Cracknell, R. (2018) *Women in Parliament and Government*, House of Commons Library. Available at: https://researchbriefings.parliament.uk/ResearchBriefing/Summary/SN01250 (accessed 14 July 2018).

Kings College London (2018) *Julia Gillard Establishes Global Institute for Women's Leadership at King's College London*, April [Online]. Available at: www.kcl.ac.uk/sspp/policy-institute/news/newsrecords/2018/julia-gillard-establishes-global-institute-for-women's-leadership-at-king's-college-london.aspx (accessed 14 July 2018).

Korica, M. (2018) *Difficult Women*. Available at: https://medium.com/@maja.korica/some-reflections-on-the-subject-of-difficult-women-cdcb6781ecb2 (accessed 14 July 2018).

Mahdawi, A. (2017) 'Allow me to womansplain the problem with gendered language', *The Guardian*, 23 April [Online]. Available at: www.theguardian.com/commentisfree/2017/apr/23/allow-me-to-womans-plain-the-problem-with-gendered-language (accessed 14 July 2018).

McKinsey (2012) *Making the Breakthrough*, Women Matter series, March [Online]. Available at: www. mckinsey.com/~/media/McKinsey/Business%20Functions/Organization/Our%20Insights/Women%20 matter/Women_matter_mar2012_english%20(1).ashx (accessed 14 July 2018).

Oksman, O. (2016) 'Are gendered toys harming childhood development?' *The Guardian*, 28 May [Online]. Available at: www.theguardian.com/lifeandstyle/2016/may/28/toys-kids-girls-boys-childhood-develop ment-gender-research (accessed 14 July 2018).

Oxford Reference (2018) *Carl Gustav Jung* [Online]. Available at: www.oxfordreference.com/view/10.1093/ oi/authority.20110803100027254 (accessed 15 July 2018).

Pankhurst, K. (2016) *Fantastically Great Women Who Changed the World*. London: Bloomsbury.

Rice, C. (2013) 'How blind auditions help orchestras to eliminate gender bias', *The Guardian*, 14 October [Online]. Available at: www.theguardian.com/women-in-leadership/2013/oct/14/blind-auditions-orches tras-gender-bias (accessed 14 July 2018).

Rivera, J. (2016) 'Why is *Star Wars* merchandise missing the hero of *The Force Awakens*?', *GQ*, January [Online]. Available at: www.gq.com/story/star-wars-toys-wheres-rey (accessed 14 July 2018).

Saujani, R. (2106) 'Teach girls bravery, not perfection', *TED*, February 2016 [Online]. Available at: www. youtube.com/watch?v=fC9da6eqaqg (accessed 19 October 2018).

Schumpeter (2014) 'The look of a leader', *The Economist*, 27 September [Online]. Available at: www.econ omist.com/business/2014/09/27/the-look-of-a-leader (accessed 14 July 2018).

Smith, D.G., Nikolov, M.C. and Rosenstein, J.E. (2018a) 'The different words we use to describe male and female leaders', *Harvard Business Review*, 25 May [Online]. Available at: https://hbr.org/2018/05/the-dif ferent-words-we-use-to-describe-male-and-female-leaders%20-%20Smith,%20Rosenstein,%20Nicolov (accessed 14 July 2018).

Smith, D.G., Rosenstein, J.E., Nikolov, M.C. and Chaney, D.A. (2018b) 'The power of language: Gender, status, and agency in performance evaluations', *Sex Roles*, 80(3–4): 159–171, May [Online]. https://link.springer. com/article/10.1007%2Fs11199-018-0923-7 (accessed 15 January 2019).

Sturgeon, N. (2017) *An Lanntair's programme in celebration of International Women's Day*, March [Online]. Available at: http://lanntair.com/nicola-sturgeon-speech-international-womens-day/ (accessed 15 July 2018).

Tickle, L. (2018) 'Language in school job ads puts women off headteacher roles', *The Guardian*, 19 June [Online]. Available at: www.theguardian.com/education/2018/jun/19/language-school-headteacher- job-ads-puts-women-off (accessed 15 July 2018).

Turner, C. (2017) 'Women make up less than a quarter of UK boardrooms', *The Guardian*, 27 March [Online]. Available at: www.theguardian.com/sustainable-business/2017/mar/27/women-make-up-less- than-a-quarter-of-uk-boardrooms (accessed 14 July 2018).

University of Oxford Careers Service (2015) *Sixth-form Girls Less Career Confident than Boys, which Can Affect the Types of Jobs they Secure*, University of Oxford, November [Online]. Available at: www.ox.ac. uk/news/2015-11-24-sixth-form-girls-less-career-confident-boys-which-can-affect-types-jobs-they-secure (accessed 14 July 2018).

Victoria State Government (n.d.) *Respectful Relationships: A Resource Kit for Victorian Schools* [Online]. Available at: http://fuse.education.vic.gov.au/Resource/ByPin?Pin=LFZGD2&SearchScope=All (accessed 14 July 2018).

Williams, Z. (2018) 'What's the best way to get written out of history? Be a middle-aged woman', *The Guardian*, 11 April [Online]. Available at: www.theguardian.com/world/2018/apr/11/whats-the-best-way- to-get-written-out-of-history-be-a-middle-aged-woman (accessed 15 July 2018).

WISE (2017) *The STEM Education Pipeline 2017*. Available at: www.wisecampaign.org.uk/statistics/ the-stem-education-pipeline-2017/ (accessed 14 July 2018).

INTERNATIONAL PERSPECTIVES

LIZ FREE

KEY POINTS

This chapter will:

- Highlight the growth and development of #WomenEd throughout the world

- Consider women's leadership and the global education landscape

- Identify ways to develop women leaders for the future needs of our growing global education community

INTRODUCTION

If you educate a woman, you educate a family, if you educate a girl, you educate the future.

Queen Rania of Jordan, 2015

In 2015 Queen Rania of Jordan joined forces with America's first lady, Michelle Obama, to bring global attention to the #LetGirlsLearn initiative. With 98 million girls worldwide not in school, this initiative aimed to help adolescent girls attain a quality education and came from the premise that all girls should have the opportunity to gain the skills, knowledge and confidence to break the cycle of poverty, raise healthier families and help build their communities. Considering the 1948 United Nations Universal Declaration of Human Rights Article 26 stated that 'everyone has the right to education' (UN General Assembly, 1948), we have made limited progress and the gender issues continue to loom large. Access to education from a global view identifies a gender disparity that is also replicated in the universal and global disparity of the underrepresentation of women in school leadership (Organisation for Economic Co-operation and Development (OECD), 2014). Women dominate the education workforce but do not break through to equitable representation in leadership, and not much has changed in the past decade.

This chapter will explore some of the challenges faced throughout the world for our young women, our teachers and our school leaders. It will take a snapshot view of the global landscape and will then dive into country-specific perspectives of #WomenEd networks internationally. We will identify role models for our community who embody the very essence of our movement and who are leading reform. In looking through a magnifying glass and focusing on the experiences of women leaders in education in a range of countries, we can start to identify common themes where the #WomenEd values are not only relevant but critical to forming a common universal language for reflection, discourse and action.

#WomenEd is truly an international movement with a rapidly growing number of networks across the world. The rise of this global network, through new and immediate channels of communication such as Twitter and Facebook, enables us to make more connections, to learn more from each other and to truly make a difference for our current and future leaders for the benefit of young people throughout the world. We now have the opportunity, the channels, the dynamic network and the language to drive global change as we strive for global equality.

THE GLOBAL VIEW

Gender inequality is not only a pressing moral and social issue but also a critical economic challenge. If women – who account for half the world's population – do not achieve their full economic potential, the global economy will suffer. (Woetzel et al., 2015)

Globally, the education profession is dominated by women (OECD, 2017). Over two-thirds are women and yet women in education leadership account for less than half of school leadership. This demonstrates a significant global gender disparity from women in teaching to women in education leadership.

The proportional bias towards women is most visible in pre-primary and primary education, where approximately 8 out of 10 teachers are women (OECD, 2014). These differences are also evident in secondary education, where across OECD member countries 68% of teachers are women, but 49% of principals in lower secondary education are women. While this means that on average every second principal is female, it does mean that women are less likely to progress from teaching into strategic school leadership roles. There is also some wide variation in countries. For example, 68% of Korean teachers are female whereas only 13% of Korean principals are women. In Finland and Portugal, 7 out of 10 teachers are women but approximately only 4 out of 10 principals are. On the other hand, in Norway, 61% of teachers and 58% of principals are women, and in Poland the gender gap is below 10%. The global table on principals in lower secondary education shows the full picture (OECD, 2014).

Much has been written within domestic systems about why we're not seeing proportional progression from teaching roles into leadership roles. However, there is limited research from a global perspective, and we need more. In a 'Spotlight' report in 2015, OECD ask, 'why are women not found in the position of school leader more often, given that they make up the majority of the teaching force?', and conclude:

> Certainly, many factors determine the number of female principals in a country. The education and skill level of candidates, individual willingness to take up the role of principal, the number of female applicants, as well as gender-bias in perceptions of leadership ability play an important role. Changing these obstacles requires systemic efforts that go beyond the individual hiring process. While providing hiring boards that select principals with clearer guidelines or gender targets can be a first step towards increasing representation of women in school leadership positions, more can and should be done to decrease other sources of potential bias or barriers to female leadership. (OECD, 2015: 7)

So, what does this mean and why is it important to increase gender representation from the teaching profession into education leadership? Apart from the substantial political, social and moral imperative for gender equality that the McKinsey Global Institute report identifies (Woetzel et al., 2015), we quite simply cannot meet the future and expected demand for education without harnessing the potential for education leadership from within the education workforce. The world's population reached nearly 7.6 billion in mid-2017 (UN, 2017). Current estimates indicate that roughly 83 million people are being added to the world's population every year, with the global population being expected to reach 8.6 billion in 2030, 9.8 billion in 2050 and 11.2 billion in 2100. This is staggering global growth, almost a doubling of population in a century. This challenges the fundamental principles behind education entitlement and the economic potential that is predicated on educated societies. Do we have the education leadership capacity in place to respond to these increasing needs?

This challenge is not only a growing future challenge, but also one we face in the here and now as we continue the movement towards greater parity and access to education throughout the world as a fundamental human right. Young people already account for about one out of every six people worldwide (UN, 2018). By 2030 the number of youth is projected to have grown by 7%, to nearly 1.3 billion; over half of this growth will be in Africa, followed by Asia. The United Nations Department for Economic and Social Affairs describe this challenge:

> Among the greatest challenges facing many countries today are inadequate human capital investment and high unemployment rates among youth. Some countries are struggling currently to educate and employ their young people, while also anticipating substantial growth in the number of youth. These countries will be doubly challenged in their efforts to assure universal high-quality education, productive employment and decent work for all. (UN, 2015: 1)

Education is at the very heart of this conundrum and even before we hit continued growth, we are already struggling to keep up. The UN assert that 'education systems of many countries are leaving behind a substantial proportion of the population' (UN, 2015: 2). We already have 32 countries where fewer than 80% of 15–24-year-olds are literate. Of these 32 countries, 18 are projected to see a more than 40% increase in the number of youth between 2015 and 2030. With urgency, we need to galvanise all the expertise we have within the profession to address the challenges our populations face. The two-thirds of our global profession who are women are therefore crucial to the national and international conversation about how we can rethink education to meet the growing economic, social and moral challenges that we face. They need a seat at the table and, if this is not offered, they need to bring their own (thank you Meghan Markle, who made this very point in her capacity as a UN women's advocate).

We need to fully utilise the potential of our teaching base to ensure a full and representative supply of expertise for education leadership. This starts with harnessing the potential of our women within the profession to ensure we can meet the global education demand. To address this as a global issue, the conversation needs to bring together learning and research from across the world. #WomenEd is a catalyst that is starting to provide a space and vehicle for this endeavour; joining the threads, identifying the trends, and working together for future global security and prosperity for the benefit of all.

@WOMENED_US

CONTRIBUTOR: MARY BRIDGET BURNS

What comes to mind when you hear the words 'American teacher'? For many, the phrase brings the image of a woman, and often a white woman, to mind. Indeed, according to the National Center for Educational Statistics, in 2011–2012, 82% of public school teachers were white and 76% of teachers were female, a statistic that increases depending on the survey used and the age level taught. Despite their dominance in the teaching field, women comprise only about 20% of superintendents and 50% of high school principals. They are woefully underrepresented on panels of education experts and policy-making boards. The disparity is even worse for women of colour.

US women who are public school teachers have benefited from well-established unions at the national and state levels. The historic 2018 teacher strikes in the states of

(Continued)

(Continued)

West Virginia, Kentucky, Oklahoma and elsewhere were dominated by women practitioners with support from unions, but the need for grassroot conversations about educational issues remains. Teachers are eager to share their thoughts and ideas, to connect beyond their individual schools to fellow educators across the globe.

@WomenEd_US provides platforms for the voices of women educators through sponsored Twitter chats, blog posts and academic research contributions. The group is quickly becoming a significant contributor to the discussion of American education by helping women educators share their insights and encourage one another to pursue leadership positions.

Twitter chats have been successful in raising key questions and engaging the community. Dr Rosa Perez-Isiah (@RosaIsiah) curated #WeLeadEd with a series of questions including: 'Q1 If women are making gains in school leadership (according to The National Center for Education Statistics (the NCES), almost 50% of principals are women), what is keeping them from district leadership?' This forum is open and accessible to all, and this one tweet alone received 95 engagements online.

The @WomenEd_US movement is currently guided by a steering committee comprised of women educators from around the US, from the East Coast to the Midwest to the South and the Southwest. They represent a variety of racial, linguistic, cultural and geographic backgrounds. They are school board members, university professors, teachers and researchers. They juggle caring for aging parents, young children, career advancement and finding meaningful work. Through their involvement in @WomenEd_US, the national steering team and followers have found an inviting, authentic and supportive community that is dedicated to raising each other up however possible.

By creating a virtual space that is welcoming and authentic, @WomenEd_US members have made this branch of #WomenEd uniquely American. The monthly Twitter chats cover topics like leadership, work–life balance, confidence, overcoming social structural barriers such as misogyny or racism, and the use of research. Since its inception in the States, @WomenEd_US has observed significant political and policy changes that have had major impacts on education. Together as a group, @WomenEd_US has navigated new policies, pressures and politics of the present day by slowly changing the tenor of the national conversation. This does not mean that all members agree on all topics, nor does the @WomenEd_US group try to police views. Rather, it is a fellowship that comes with many viewpoints, but a shared mission: to lift the voices of all women educators, so that their views may be heard and respected; to give them confidence and strength; to encourage them to be just 10% braver, so that they may be better able to reach their goals.

THE DUTCH DILEMMA

CONTRIBUTORS: LIZ FREE, SUE ASPINALL AND SANDRA DE BRESSER

The Netherlands is a contradiction in so many ways. It consistently ranks in the top 10 of the world's happiest nations, Dutch children are considered to be the happiest in the world (Adamson, 2013) and the education system is high performing. The average student scored 508 in reading literacy, maths and science in the OECD's Programme for International Student Assessment (PISA). This score is higher than the average of 486. This also makes the Netherlands one of the highest performing countries in students' skills. On average, girls outperformed boys by 6 points, more than the average gap of 2 points (OECD, 2016).

The Netherlands also has the lowest rate of working long hours; just 0.5% of employees working long hours against the average of 13%. Many Dutch families share work responsibilities – the female employment rate of 69.9% is well above the average of 57.5%, as are maternal employment rates. However, women predominantly work part time and spend almost two hours more per day working within the home than men. And now we begin to explore the Dutch dichotomy of proportionally high outcomes for wellbeing, education, women working and flexible working against some of the highest gender gaps in education leadership across the world: the Dutch dilemma.

The role of women in the workplace has seen a dramatic shift in the past 40 years. In the early '80s the female employment rate was among the lowest in the OECD at around 35%. However, by 2009 it had doubled to over 70%. Much of the increase in female employment has been on a part-time basis, with over 61% of employed women working part time, which is particularly prevalent among employed mothers and reflected throughout education. The OECD identifies that this trend 'may free up time for family commitments, but often has negative consequences on career progression and underutilises women's education and skills' (OECD, n.d.[b]). The data speaks for itself. Young Dutch women are more educated than the OECD average, and more educated than young Dutch men. However, a working mother with two grown-up children has, on average, earned less than half of the total working-life earnings of otherwise similar female employees.

Against this national backdrop and like the majority of other countries, most of the teaching workforce in the Netherlands is female at all levels of education (it should be noted that within this, we have the highest share of male teachers in pre-primary education of all OECD countries, 13% compared to an average of 3%). The proportion of women teachers in primary sits at 86.2%. This falls to an average of 65.7% for women teachers in primary through to tertiary education (OECD, 2016). Yet despite this, the Netherlands' record for women in education leadership is among the lowest reported in the world, second only to Japan and Korea (OECD, 2014). Rather surprisingly, and against the Dutch success of high-quality work–life balance, increased numbers of women working and national policies encouraging part-time family-friendly policies, women are significantly underrepresented in education leadership roles: they make up only 30.8% of lower secondary principals, which is considerably lower than the average of 45% and below of our colleagues in the UK, the USA and the Czech Republic, to name but a few. It is a dramatic and somewhat disappointing reality against a national picture that has been increasingly bright for women.

In January 2017, and in response to this picture, a small group of women leaders based in The Hague met to ponder how we could nurture, develop and strengthen women in Dutch education leadership. We looked at the #WomenEd movement alongside the Netherlands data and quickly realised that many of the challenges were the same. We recognised the same fundamental issues faced by our UK colleagues and felt an affinity with the #WomenEd mission:

(Continued)

(Continued)

> Even though women dominate the workforce across all sectors of education there still remain gender inequalities, particularly at senior leadership level . . . This situation is clearly unacceptable and rapid change is needed. #WomenEd will therefore campaign and use its collective power to make improvements, so that there is a more equitable balance in terms of gender and ethnicity at leadership level across all sectors of education. (#WomenEd, 2015)

With this, @WomenEdNL was born on International Women's Day, 2017. With a growing community of over 200 education leaders involved in the @WomenEdNL network, the organisation is beginning to mirror the grassroots development in the UK.

Our first #LeadMeet brought together over 50 educators, and four bold and brave women leaders took an unknown step and shared their stories. It was inspirational. One attendee, Vicky (@VickyFoulkes), shared in her tweet to the speakers, 'Thank you to the brave and bold speakers @WomenEdNL this is just what I needed! #BeBoldForChange', and another attendee, Karen, @MsB_NL, tweeted 'Some brave personal recounts and an inspiring message—stand up and #BeBoldForChange @WomenEd @WomenEdNL'. Not only did they come en masse to the first event, way beyond our expectations, but they then kept coming. Not only was #WomenEd needed in the Netherlands, but it continues to be needed as it grows and expands.

The journey has been rapid from the first session to the present. We have termly #LeadMeets, alongside social occasions. Social media platforms for sharing practice, knowledge and information are firmly established. For the first time, we are communicating, connecting, collaborating, challenging and driving the #timeforchange agenda in what is often a fragmented and disconnected community between domestic and international schools. The apparent polarity of part-time working and education leadership is at the very heart of this agenda as we work to protect the strengths of working flexibility with the systemic development and deployment of women in leadership roles. We are building confidence and an extensive community to begin rethinking how we work, how we can build on the exceptional strengths of the Dutch approach to work whilst also ensuring that we utilise the capacity that our women teachers can bring to education leadership in the Netherlands.

@WOMENEDCANADA

CONTRIBUTORS: SHELLEY L MAGNUSSON AND CAROL CAMPBELL

@WomenEdCanada was officially launched on 9 April 2017, at a dedicated pre-conference day for the annual uLead conference hosted by the Alberta Teachers' Association (ATA)

Council for School Leadership. The genesis of @WomenEdCanada, however, goes back a couple of years. At the 2015 uLead conference it was noticed that there were no women keynote speakers. One of the speakers invited women to take his seat on the main stage, and the process towards ensuring women's leadership and representation at future events began.

In 2016 the first women's one-day pre-conference was organised. During that pre-conference, delegates noted that women's leadership was something that needed to become a permanent feature of uLead. In 2017, a group of women from Alberta, Ontario, Australia and the UK came together to organise the women's pre-conference, to present various workshops throughout the main conference and to be part of a panel on women's leadership in education. By this time #WomenEd had emerged in the UK, and we decided to join forces with the #WomenEd founders to draw on their 8C values of clarity, communication, connection, confidence, collaboration, community, challenge and change. These encouraged women to give voice to the realities that women were facing in their own work environments. Approximately 100 people participated in the @WomenEdCanada pre-conference. This work was continued in the panel discussion at uLead where @WomenEdCanada was launched. We challenged the 1,200 members of the audience to grow our group and shared with them the goal of 1,000 followers by the end of the year. By the end of the four-day conference, we had already exceeded our goal. And thus @WomenEdCanada was born.

Issues of gender equity, including access to careers, promotions and pay, are gaining prominence in Canada. The current Prime Minister announced a gender-balanced Cabinet 'because it's 2015', and in both of the home provinces of the authors, Alberta and Ontario, the Premiers (highest political office) are currently female. However, despite prominent leaders and political commitments, gender equity on the ground has not yet been fully realised.

As of 2015, in Canada 84% of elementary teachers were women, but only 45% of principals were women. At the high school level, the disparity is more pronounced, with women making up 59% of the teaching profession but only 27% are principals. In Alberta, 74% of teachers are women while only 41% are principals. In Alberta School Board's Association, only 11 out of 61 superintendents are women. In Ontario, the majority of elementary vice principals/principals are now women; however, while 81% of elementary teachers are women, only 65% of vice principals/principals are women. By contrast, 19% of elementary teachers are men yet 35% of vice principals/principals are men. Women in school leadership positions also tend to have considerably longer professional experience compared with men. The issue, therefore, is not simply asking how many women are education leaders, it is the balance of who gets promoted in a predominantly female profession and based on what criteria and experience.

In Canada, we are loath to even contemplate the idea of quotas for women in leadership, even though quotas have proven to be very successful in other countries. Ulrike Lunacek, former European Parliament Vice President, speaking at the Education International World Women's Conference on 7 February 2018, suggested that society and unions also need structures to support women – and that quotas are also needed. She said: 'To the women who say they don't want to be a quota woman, I say "How many men are in their positions just because they are men, not because they are the best?" We

(Continued)

(Continued)

need quotas to get women into leadership positions and keep them there, and so girls can see role models and we can change things.'

The fact that women do occupy leadership positions shows that there is no absolute barrier to women's advancement. There are, however, institutional and societal barriers that form a labyrinth that women must navigate that is vastly different from the obstacles that men face. @WomenEdCanada provides a network to support women navigating the challenges and complexities of becoming and being education leaders.

@WOMENEDCZECH

CONTRIBUTOR: EMILY RANKIN

Ever heard of Františka Plamínková? Born in 1875, she was a Czech teacher, feminist and suffragist in a time when teachers were forbidden from marrying and women couldn't vote. She went on to serve as Senate Chair in the National Assembly and the Vice President of the International Council of Women, among other things. I'd like to think she'd be pleased by the efforts of the #WomenEd movement and decry the gender inequality that exists in the Czech education profession today.

According to the OECD's Teaching and Learning International Survey (TALIS), the Czech Republic has one of the highest percentages of female teachers in OECD and partner countries at 76.5%, yet school leadership is only 48% female, most being in primary schools with pay lower than that of males leading secondary institutions. Furthermore, this female-dominated teaching workforce is underpaid when compared with like nations; teachers with 15 years of experience earn salaries that rank 30th out of 33 surveyed (OECD, n.d.[a]).

It seems the landscape here would be ripe for change, but, as Czech students and friends relay, 'feminism' is a contested concept, often dismissed as an over-dramatised notion that doesn't fit easily into a culture with airtight gender roles and a gross under-representation of women in politics and commerce. Thus, change is certainly a challenge.

This is where @WomenEdCzech comes in. The branch is fledgling; we held our first official meeting in January 2018, with a small team of expatriate educators from international schools in Prague. Since then we've tweeted in Czech and reached out to a number of Czech schools to invite them to our first event; we are committed to connecting with our native Czech counterparts and hope to gain more steam by holding an unconference. We recognise the problematic nature of our current fully expatriate core, who are paid a more internationally comparable wage. Still, not one of the schools we work in is led by a woman, and maternity benefits are wholly underwhelming, or non-existent, in some. We all have a lot to gain by collaborating.

Our first event was all about communicating the #WomenEd mission to attendees and workshopping ways to confidently express our voices, especially in male-dominated situations and matters of negotiation. The very presence of the event itself invited engagement with the #WomenEd mission and started a dialogue in our community. @LearnCAB tweeted 'Great afternoon with some wonderful people heightening our confidence and amplifying our voice. @WomenEdCzech #WomenEd #empowerall'.

Our priority moving forward is to identify ways to develop more collaboration between women across schools and challenge ourselves to try new things; the success of a timetabling session at a #WomenEd event in the UK was particularly inspiring and we hope to have one here. Ultimately, we aim to create a community of women who have the opportunity to enact change in their respective schools and careers, with the confidence to pursue their goals.

GLOBAL ORGANISATIONAL PERSPECTIVES

The journey in writing this chapter and bringing colleagues together from across the world has highlighted the universal and global challenges that we face. Whilst female representation in education leadership is a complex and multifaceted issue, there are consistent themes that interweave the domestic pictures and the global landscape in the drive for equality and increased representation of women in education leadership throughout the world. Quite simply, women are consistently not making it through to leadership roles in education at every level. This has significant global consequences as we underutilise the very workforce that we desperately need to service the growing world population.

The challenge we face is not insurmountable. We have a baseline, the beginning seeds of action and a global conversation. #WomenEd has become a unifying vehicle for dialogue and action as we can now have clarity over the consistent themes and challenges that are a barrier to us providing all children around the world with a quality of education to which they are entitled. So, what's next and how do we build on the #WomenEd catalyst? There are several urgent actions that will enable us to build solid global foundations.

First, we need to know our community and reach out through the channels available throughout the world. This is an opportunity to identify advocates for women leadership in education and start to build a global database for our community to connect. We can take ownership for building a global network of advocates, policy influencers, mentors and coaches that can start to have an impact on practice. From this dynamic resource, we can develop a global strategy led by these incredible and visible pioneers for women education leadership.

Second, we need to look towards the rapidly growing international school market that has an extensive global network beyond arbitrary country barriers and borders. As a significant international sector throughout the full age phases in education, it can influence and develop policies and practice that can not only influence the international schools' communities, but also influence the countries in which they operate throughout the world. They can bring together global research, policy and practice for the benefit of all.

Why international schools? Well, ignoring their reach globally, the rapidly growing size and influence of this market is hugely significant. ISC Research has tracked the market since 1994 and at the COBIS conference in 2018 they published their data and projections for the next decade (ISC, 2018). As of 1 September 2017, there were 9,173 international schools servicing 4.96 million students and employing 458,000 staff. The growth has been exponential, having been just 2,584 schools in 2000. Not only has it seen incredible growth, but ISC Research is now projecting

16,400 schools servicing 10.6 million students and requiring 952,000 staff within the next decade. This global industry will be worth $43.5 billion by 2027. By any stretch of the imagination, this is not an insignificant amount and affords us an opportunity to utilise this substantial market to research, develop practice and then lead the way for global reform. As an aside, there aren't enough teachers in the whole of the UK, Australia and South Africa, the traditional countries for international school teacher recruitment, to service this market. We need to be thinking differently and ensuring that we optimise the potential of the teaching workforce at every level and across the gender gap.

This growing international school market is serviced and supported by a range of organisations that provide accreditation and membership to these communities of schools. These include organisations like the Council for British International Schools (COBIS), the Council of Independent Schools (CIS), the Education Collaborative for International Schools (ECIS) and The Middle States Association Commissions on Elementary and Secondary Schools (MSA-CESS) alongside programme providers such as the International Baccalaureate Organisation (IBO). With thousands of membership schools throughout the world, and of course these numbers are increasing, these organisations have the scope and breadth to research approaches, to model best practice in their organisations and activities, and to provide an advisory role to their international schools. This can be achieved through three key areas:

1. *Understand the issues.* In researching the global perspective for women education leadership, I have found it difficult to navigate the research field to have a clear current view of the international landscape. Simply, there isn't a current universal research base in this field. The time is now ripe for our international schools' community to take the lead and to commission research, ideally starting with the best evidence synthesis of existing research. This would identify the areas for further research and enable us to develop an evidence-informed strategic approach at a global level to ensure that we have the leadership capacity required for up-and-coming and future generations.

2. *Model best practice.* It would be a bold move forwards for the organisations leading and supporting our community to model the practices that break down the gender divide and optimise the potential of the full workforce. Publicising and evidencing how each organisation is developing equality, inclusivity and diversity within their own organisations and through their activities would be a significant step forward.

3. *Advisory role.* International schools look to their membership communities and accreditation bodies for advice and support at all levels of school leadership, governance and development. Using an evidence-informed base, these organisations can develop advisory materials, support and compliance requirements for schools to promote equality, diversity and inclusive practice for optimal workforce planning and deployment, particularly at a time when staff supply to meet the global demands will become a major challenge.

Galvanising the international education community into action is the opportunity that this generation can take for the benefit of us now and the future generations of educators and students. Gloria Macapagal Arroyo, Former President of the Philippines, said 'the power of one, if fearless and focused, is formidable, but the power of many working together is better' (2003). We need the power of one, and the power of many. In thinking about the one and the many, I thought long and hard about the woman that I would celebrate in this chapter on global perspectives. And there were many individuals over the decades, generations and millennia that I could have chosen. However, one stands out to me because she is an excellent leader of an organisation working towards a better world, where we celebrate and develop the potential of all, regardless of race, faith or gender. She is a fabulous woman too!

ROLE MODEL: DR SIVA KUMARI, DIRECTOR GENERAL, INTERNATIONAL BACCALAUREATE

Dr Siva Kumari was appointed seventh Director General of the International Baccalaureate (IB) in January 2014, becoming the first internal candidate and woman to hold the post. In 2018, the IB, which offers education programmes to more than one million students in 153 countries worldwide, celebrated 50 years as a multinational, not-for-profit foundation, focused on delivering excellent education for learners aged 3-19.

I have chosen Dr Kumari as a role model for women in leadership globally because she continues to have an incredibly successful career as a leader of education across the world and she is driven by a core mission, vision and purpose for inclusive global education. She is committed and dedicated to education for all as a vehicle for global betterment. Dr Kumari is a beacon of aspiration and inspiration, and I admire her. This sense of purpose is best read in her own words:

> I cherish the IB's rich history and its mission, built on the belief that education can create a better world – and should be available to all, regardless of where they live, their socio-economic background or gender. Good education should be possible in all settings.
>
> We are putting human development in teachers' hands, so that students can perform to the very best of their abilities, and therefore we need to remove barriers so they can fully develop our next generation of humanity. This will only work if education becomes truly inclusive. The IB is committed to this – and has been since it was founded in 1968. We have always been an innovative, restless organisation, ceaselessly working to improve, and inclusion and diversity have always been seen as essential to our mission.
>
> The IB believes that successful humans are forever curious, think critically, continue to learn and re-learn – and recognise the perspective of others. We are thankful for all the remarkable educators that make this effort each day.

In 2019, Dr Kumari is a member of the international jury who will select winners for the second Global Pluralism Award, which recognises individuals and organisations who exemplify 'pluralism in action' and are building societies where diversity is respected and valued.

Prior to joining the IB, Dr Kumari served as the first associate provost for K-12 Initiatives at Rice University, USA where she worked for 15 years. In addition to her Bachelor of Science degree, she holds a Master's degree and a Doctorate in Education.

CHANGING THE SYSTEM

Yes, it is time. Now is the moment. In joining us on this journey through global perspectives on women leadership in education throughout the world, you will have learned about the strength of community and the growth of the #WomenEd voice, and also begun to connect the challenges that are not bound by borders, exclusive to one country or another, but that are global issues that urgently need a global solution. I encourage you to consider the following:

1. Reach out; reach far and wide as we extend our community. We are a global profession. I challenge you all to make contact with a #WomenEd colleague in another country. Let's start a global conversation through collaboration and learn from one another at a grassroots level.

2. Let's find our global voice. Be loud and proud. There are many opportunities in the global education calendar to be present, to present and to be heard. Submit a session proposal, offer to speak at a global #LeadMeet, write an article or blog discussing the issues, underpinned by robust global data, and call for further research, development and action. We need to raise the profile of the gender gap in education leadership globally.

3. Hold others to account. Challenge the organisations that work alongside you in whatever role you have. Ask them about what they are doing to close the gender gap in education leadership and to optimise the potential of the profession. How are they developing, implementing and evidencing the impact of their approaches?

4. Look inwards, within your own organisation. How is this issue being addressed, how is the organisation building professional capacity to meet growing demands and what is your contribution to developing the potential of women in your immediate communities?

5. Lastly, look forwards. Look towards an inclusive global profession where we develop and utilise the potential of all. Let's capture this ideal and develop a global strategy for this aspiration through our global #WomenEd world. Let's all be that little bit braver!

REFERENCES

Adamson, P. (2013) *Child Well-being in Rich Countries*. Florence: UNICEF Office of Research - Innocenti.

ISC (2018) *The Global Report for Schools 2018*. London: ISC.

Macapagal-Arroyo, G. (2003) Vin d' Honneur Speech, January [Online]. Available at: https://www.official-gazette.gov.ph/2003/01/09/vin-d-honneur-speech-of-president-arroyo-on-meeting-the-challenges-of-change-through-unity-and-cooperation/ (accessed 4 December 2018).

OECD (2014) *TALIS 2013 Results: An International Perspective on Teaching and Learning*. Available at: https://read.oecd-ilibrary.org/education/talis-2013-results_9789264196261-en#page68 (accessed 18 July 2018).

OECD (2015) *Trends Shaping Education 2015, Spotlight 7* [Online]. Available at: www.oecd.org/education/ceri/Spotlight7-GenderEquality.pdf (accessed 18 July 2018).

OECD (2016) *OECD Economic Surveys: Netherlands 2016*. Paris: OECD Publishing. Available at: www.oecd-ilibrary.org/economics/oecd-economic-surveys-netherlands-2016_eco_surveys-nld-2016-en (accessed 18 July 2018).

OECD (2017) *Education Indicators In Focus*, February [Online]. Available at: https://read.oecd-ilibrary.org/education/gender-imbalances-in-the-teaching-profession_54f0ef95-en#page1 (accessed 18 July 2018).

OECD (n.d.[a]) *Country Profile Czech Republic* [Online]. Available at: www.oecd.org/czech/TALIS-Country-profile-Czech-Republic.pdf (accessed 18 July 2018).

OECD (n.d.[b]) *Better Life Index*. Available at: www.oecdbetterlifeindex.org/countries/netherlands/ (accessed 18 July 2018).

United Nations (2015) *World Population Prospects: The 2017 Revision, Key Findings and Advance Tables*, Department of Economic and Social Affairs, Population Division, Working Paper No. ESA/P/WP/248 [Online]. Available at: www.un.org/en/development/desa/population/publications/pdf/popfacts/PopFacts_2015-1.pdf (accessed 18 July 2018).

United Nations (2018) *Population Facts: Youth Population Trends and Sustainable Development* [Online]. Available at: www.un.org/esa/socdev/documents/youth/fact-sheets/YouthPOP.pdf (accessed 25 April 2018).

United Nations General Assembly (1948) *Universal Declaration of Human Rights*, 10 December, *217 A* (III). Available at: www.refworld.org/docid/3ae6b3712c.html (accessed 16 February 2018).

Woetzel, J., Madgavkar, A., Ellingrud, K., Labaye, E., Devillard, S., Kutcher, E., Manyika, J., Dobbs, R. and Krishnan, M. (2015) *The Power of Parity: How Advancing Women's Equality Can Add $Trillion to Global Growth*, McKinsey Global Institute report [Online]. Available at: www.mckinsey.com/global-themes/employment-and-growth/how-advancing-womens-equality-can-add-12-trillion-to-global-growth (accessed 18 July 2018).

#WomenEd (2015) *#WomenEd* [Online]. Available at: www.womened.org/ (accessed 18 July 2018).

Tweets:

@VickyFoulkes https://twitter.com/VickyFoulkes/status/838815395226218498

@LearnCab https://twitter.com/LearnCAB/status/1011240022643789824

@Rosalsiah https://twitter.com/Rosalsiah/status/1004168242930184193

@MsB_NL https://twitter.com/MsB_NL/status/838844073092001792

5

CONCRETE CEILINGS AND KINKED HOSEPIPES: UNDERSTANDING THE EXPERIENCES OF BME FEMALE LEADERS IN SCHOOLS

SAMEENA CHOUDRY

KEY POINTS

This chapter will:

- Share the experiences of 12 black and minority ethnic (BME) female heads and senior leaders in England in 2017

- Consider the barriers and enablers to becoming headteachers for these women

- Unpick the institutional and structural constraints that exist for female BME leaders

- Highlight key factors and practical changes that need to be made

INTRODUCTION

At a time when the pupil population is becoming increasingly diverse in terms of ethnicity, the equivalent representation of ethnicity and gender amongst the leadership of schools remains stubbornly low. If we genuinely want to recruit from the best talent pool available to us for leadership positions, changes need to be made. This chapter draws on the findings of qualitative research obtained from 12 black and minority ethnic (BME) female heads and senior leaders in state-funded secondary schools in England in 2017. My research used an intersectional approach (Crenshaw, 1989) with a focus on ethnicity and gender and other characteristics such as age and religion where relevant. Intersectionality tells us that the various forms of social stratification, such as class, race, sexual orientation, age, disability and gender, do not exist separately from each other but are complexly interwoven. To be a woman of ethnicity in education therefore sets up more barriers and challenges our collective unconscious further. In her book *The Education and Career of Black Teachers*, Osler (1997) warns us of the dangers of treating women as a homogeneous group. She cites Adler et al. (1993) and states:

> It is equally important in a study of black senior managers that we guard against sweeping generalisations, since they are likely to have both common and varying experiences. (1997: 115)

My research is cognisant of this fact and presents the findings within these confines. The main purpose of my research was to focus on both the barriers and the enablers that had led these women to reach the top at a time when there are increasingly growing disparities in the percentages of the number of BME pupils in our schools and the lack of commensurate representation of BME teachers and leaders. I drew on the seminal work of Osler (1997) and that of Bush et al. (2005) on BME leaders, and McNamara et al. (2010), Coleman (2005, 2007) and Fuller (2017) on women leaders in schools, and focused on the participants' experience. They faced structural and personal barriers whilst also celebrating the enablers that supported their success. The chapter ends with a series of questions for you and the organisations in which you work. I hope these questions prompt you to consider how they apply to your own context and what you can do to bring about positive change.

CONCRETE CEILINGS

The Department for Education's (DfE) 2016 data shows that only 3.1% of heads in schools are from BME backgrounds compared to the pupil population of 31.4% in primary and 27.9% of secondary.

In 2015, the National Union of Teachers wrote to every headteacher in England and Wales asking them to ensure that their teaching staff reflected the communities they serve. The union warned that in the majority of schools 'the only black role models were administrative staff, cleaners, kitchen or security staff' and were concerned that this would 'impact negatively on the achievement of black children as they do not see representations that can act as role models for them to aim to achieve at a higher level' (Garner, 2015).

The particular needs of BME women have been articulated by Nicole Haynes, a secondary headteacher in London, in a blog for Ambition School Leadership: 'In 2016, there is still a gender bias against women in secondary school headships. Often, interview panels and governing bodies are not ethnically, or gender balanced, enabling sexism and racism to come into play (sometimes) unconsciously and unchallenged.'

The barrier to women becoming headteachers is often likened to a glass ceiling, and in exploring the factors that limited the numbers of BME women senior leaders in schools I would argue that the barrier is stronger and far harder to break through. The ceiling for BME leaders is not made of glass but of concrete.

I initially collected data through a qualitative open-ended questionnaire, followed by semi-structured one-to-one interviews with 10 of the 12 leaders (4 current heads and 6 aspirant heads of the future). The heads or aspirant heads interviewed were all from state-funded second-ary schools. As a female of BME background and a former senior leader in schools with significant experience of working with heads and senior leaders across all phases, the intention was that this would limit the effect of the impact of the 'observer' who is an 'outsider' (Gunaratnam, 2003).

The questionnaire included questions under the following sections:

- background details, career history and progression
- barriers and enablers to leadership
- details of experience and perceptions of BME careers in education and leadership with a focus on intersectionality
- actions that would help BME teachers in achieving their leadership aspirations

An analysis of the findings offers an insight into the key barriers to and enablers of achieving leadership success.

BARRIERS

Common barriers to success identified by respondents include attitudes towards BME teach-ers, caring and family responsibilities and being young. In addition, factors such as social and cultural issues, lack of professional networks, and workload were also cited. However, the top three most commonly cited were lack of self-confidence, availability of suitable posts, and atti-tudes of senior leaders displaying covert racism and sexism, and I'll focus on these.

Lack of self-confidence was one of the recurring themes found in my research, and this builds on the findings of Coleman (2007) when looking into gender inequalities. She compared head-teachers' views on gender and leadership eight years apart and found that over this period very little had changed, with women, in general, taking less time and opportunities to carefully plan their careers, especially for senior roles, compared to men. In addition, some seemed to lack confidence in applying for senior roles compared to their male counterparts. What was inter-esting in my research was that the respondents who raised this as an issue were very self-aware and reflective that this was a limiting factor with which they had to grapple: on a few occasions this had been pointed out to them by others who were supporting them on their leadership journey. Even though some likened this lack of confidence to a 'disease', on a positive note, they decided to go ahead and apply for leadership positions even though self-doubt still lingered.

Coleman (2007) also highlighted that women in general tend to over-prepare as a strategy to compensate for their lack of self-confidence. In several cases the respondents I interviewed highlighted that they did this and worked much harder as a result, acknowledging that they probably did put in more time and effort than needed. This is an important issue that needs addressing, particularly at a time when excessive workload and stress are prevalent within teach-ing and are often cited as reasons for leaving the profession. A recent survey undertaken by the

NFER (Lynch and Worth, 2017) highlighted that the retention rate among secondary heads has fallen from 91% in 2012 to 87% in 2015. Women putting extra stress and work on themselves is an additional barrier that is not conducive to the wellbeing of individuals. Our #WomenEd values of confidence, collaboration and community recognise these issues and provide opportunities for women to garner the support of a wider community that recognises and helps to resolve these matters in a realistic, collective manner.

The availability of suitable posts was highlighted as one of the top three barriers for female leaders by MacNamara et al. (2008) more than 20 years ago. This was still seen as a barrier for the women in my study. Almost all the respondents felt that there were a limited number of posts available to them. This, I believe, is further exacerbated in secondary education where there are fewer schools and hence opportunities, unless you are willing to move out of your geographical vicinity. This is particularly the case for headship posts. Based on the findings of my research, those who had succeeded in gaining promotion had primarily done so because an opportunity had arisen in the school in which they were already working or very close by so that they could commute. If these opportunities had not come up, it was unlikely that they would have sought similar positions further afield; the education system would have been deprived of their leadership skills and their own careers would have stalled. There were, however, notable exceptions to this. One respondent had relocated a considerable distance and lived at a new workplace during the week, returning home over 200 miles away at weekends. In doing so, she had made an impressive contribution to turning around a school previously labelled as 'failing' to 'good', in Ofsted terms, in a relatively short period of time as a new head, thereby demonstrating her considerable leadership skills. She saw this as something that could be done for a short period of time and planned to move to a job closer to home when the opportunity allowed, especially once her leadership capabilities had been demonstrated by improving that school. Another had relocated with her partner and gained promotion, with further promotion in the pipeline. However, both cited that this had been at considerable expense to their work–life balance and their families, with others stating that relocating would be more difficult to do when they had children who were settled in schools, or had other caring responsibilities. This barrier is significant and #WomenEd is aware that creative and solution-focused means of overcoming this are required. There is a need to challenge and change the system, as outlined in our #WomenEd values. Opportunities need to be created for BME women to practise and demonstrate their leadership skills and be in a strong position to apply for leadership positions when they come up locally.

The limiting and negative attitudes of senior leaders were a significant barrier in some of the respondents' leadership journeys. At times, other senior leaders acted in both racist and sexist ways. One respondent shared her experience of how a senior male leader had said in a 'joking manner' that there was little point in promoting her, and indeed other women who were of childbearing age, as they would just leave to go and have babies. They heard the message that there were few opportunities available to them in that school whilst he was there, and indeed felt that there was no alternative but for them to leave if they wanted promotion, even though they knew this was against the law. They did not want to work in a school that voiced this sort of negative, sexist culture. It was not just sexism that manifested itself, but racism too. In another example shared by one of the respondents, racist comments were made by staff about the food she brought in for lunch, as well as 'jokes' and deliberate incorrect pronunciation of her name which, when challenged, were referred to as just 'banter' and 'teasing', thereby trying to legitimise unacceptable behaviour. This again resulted in the member of staff leaving the school, especially when details of her ethnicity were shared with pupils, who were told to seek her out so that she could deal with any problems they were having as she was of the same ethnicity. This respondent had chosen not to share this with pupils and they had no way of knowing this important information if other staff had not shared it with them.

In this case, once the member of staff had left the school, she felt she had no option but to alter her name so that it sounded English and, because she was of pale complexion, it would be difficult for anyone to know that she was of BME background. She did this before she started her new school and role. In her new school she felt valued and recognised for her hard work rather than being 'othered' because of her gender or ethnicity. The fact that such incidents still take place with staff is extremely disturbing and raises issues for the pupils who are taught by such teachers and leaders.

In the main, though, the BME leaders I surveyed experienced subtle, negative and exclusionary actions rather than direct discrimination. In another case the respondent felt that she knew from discussions with other senior colleagues that her 'face did not fit in with the white man's club at the top'. She knew that she had to leave and get a job in another school if she wanted to progress and did exactly that, and was now in a school that valued her as an individual and her contribution. Another respondent shared her experiences of the additional difficulties she had to face as a female BME leader with a Muslim background. She was line manager of a team of four white men who resisted many of the strategies she wanted to implement as their leader.

The barriers faced by some of the respondents in my study show that the embedded and negative attitudes towards women (Coleman, 2005, 2007; McNamara et al., 2008) and BME leaders (Bush et al., 2005; Osler 1997) are still prevalent in some of our schools, even though these were first identified by researchers many years ago. It appears that little progress has been made. Despite successive legislation, including The Equality Act 2010 which makes it unlawful to discriminate on the grounds of gender and ethnicity or for that matter other protected characteristics, those on the receiving end still face the difficulties of countering the subtle acts that take place on a regular basis. This acts as a significant barrier in their desired leadership journeys and challenges their aspiration for promotion. #WomenEd is particularly cognisant of the individual, organisational and systematic barriers that exist and the necessity to challenge and change these from an intersectional perspective if all women are going to have the opportunities to work in an equitable education system.

The aggregation of these barriers can mean that BME women have the almost impossible task of 'drilling through concrete ceilings' as opposed to shattering the glass ceiling (Loden, 1978). The 'concrete ceiling' is an apt metaphor to describe the experience female BME leaders can face in education. It is a lump of composite material that hardens over time as it sets. It acts as an immovable barrier to prevent career progression. It also prevents others from even seeing BME colleagues as leaders. Unlike the figurative 'glass ceiling', which can be shattered, BME women who wish to get to the top have to use a drill to get through the concrete, illustrating the arduous and almost impossible task that lies ahead.

ENABLERS

Fortunately, although these examples shared by respondents highlight the barriers that still exist, on a more positive note the majority felt that schools generally are becoming better places in which to work. This was also evident in research undertaken by the Runnymede Trust and the National Union of Teachers whereby 'A higher proportion of BME staff in a school was associated with respondents feeling that the school was an inclusive and welcoming environment for staff of all ethnic backgrounds' (Haque and Elliott, 2017: 5).

In contrast to the barriers, there was generally a greater consensus among respondents as to the factors that enabled career success. Four key factors were identified as being the most important enablers:

- qualifications and experience
- attitudes of senior leaders
- performance management/appraisal
- involvement in professional networks and access to continuing professional develop-ment (CPD), including fast-track leadership programmes or accessing quality coaching and mentoring

All the respondents were more than qualified for the roles they held, with most exceeding the necessary qualifications and experiences required. They had gained additional postgrad-uate qualifications such as Master's degrees and MPhils, as well as professional qualifications such as the National Professional Qualifications for Headship (NPQH) and, for senior leaders, National Professional Qualification for Senior Leaders (NPQSL). They had deliberately undertaken these additional qualifications to be 'the best qualified for the role' so that no criticism could be lev-elled against them in relation to this requirement. A basic minimum would not suffice. The respon-dents were aware of the importance of having these additional qualifications to support their application, subsequent appointment and the undertaking of their duties. This is very much in line with Osler's (1997) research. In her study she found that her respondents' desire for further study and advanced qualifications was also deliberately undertaken to outweigh any anticipat-ed discrimination they may encounter whilst undertaking the leadership role.

Osler (1997) cited that there were three main leadership routes open to BME leaders in her study if they wished to progress their careers: the special educational needs route, the race equality route or the pastoral route. Very few were given the opportunity to progress via teaching and learning or curriculum routes, which are more likely to lead to success in leadership roles. Research by Runnymede Trust and National Union of Teachers (Haque and Elliott, 2017) sadly shows that this is still often the case over 20 years later. The respondents in my study were aware of these traps of falling into a dead-end or stereotype career. They actively sought out opportunities to gain experience and credibility in roles that would give them the breadth of experience needed to be successful as a deputy head or head.

Another striking factor that played an important role in their success as a leader was having a 'significant person' who mentored and, where required, acted as a coach. In many cases this was someone who was their previous head or had held a similar role. The support and the positive relationship they had built with this person was pivotal as they empowered and encouraged the respondent to go for the top job, even when the respondent may not have considered it themselves or had been hesitant to take up the opportunity or challenge. In such situations the significant person not only encouraged them to apply, but also articulated their different per-ceptions based on their gender and shared how males in similar circumstances would behave differently and just go for the role. Their nurturing and sometimes challenging coaching con-versations spurred the respondents to think differently and go for the role in which they were successful. In many ways this is an embodiment of all the #WomenEd values coming together. As a network, we recognised from the outset that many women were more than capable of undertaking leadership roles effectively, but for those who did not have a significant person in their professional lives and who wished to embark on the next step of their leadership journey, then #WomenEd, as a collective group, would come together to empower and support women to do so.

Another factor, quite unexpectedly, that played an important role in the success of my respondents was that of performance management or appraisal. Page's (2015) research into appraisals found that judgements were generally opaque and 'less visible'. Similarly, research by Runnymede and The National Association of Schoolmasters Union of Women Teachers also found that 'decisions about performance are not always fair and equitable, and the achievements of female and BME teachers are often underrated' (Haque, 2017: 18). However, in contrast, for my respondents, performance management gave them the opportunity to shine and align their individual needs with those of their school. What happened in the case of my respondents was, as Page states, 'For those practitioners who meet their objectives, those whose teaching meets the "good or better" standard, the appraisal should ideally be a motivating experience and even be linked to progression through the pay spines' (2015: 1031). The BME leaders I surveyed were able to show their capabilities in an open and transparent manner with evidence of impact on pupils who gained good examination results.

The power and importance of networking was also seen as an enabling factor. This was an interesting point, as in many cases, although the respondents were fully aware of the benefits of being part of a network, they often felt an 'outsider' to the traditional networks that they felt were available in education. The education community on Twitter was providing alternative ways to build networks with a wide range of educational professionals. Both #WomenEd for aspiring and existing women leaders, and #DiverseEducators, which was formed to celebrate and promote educators from a wide range of characteristics, were singled out as being of support. Both were formed on Twitter and were viewed by one respondent as an alternative to an 'old boy's network', thereby creating opportunities for those who were not white, male or middle class.

Finally, having access to high-quality continuing professional development was also important. The respondents highlighted the beneficial outcomes of fast-track programmes such as 'Talented Leaders', and leadership programmes such as the NPQH and the NPQSL. All respondents felt that they had benefited considerably from such professional learning opportunities.

ORGANISATIONAL PERSPECTIVES: KINKED HOSEPIPES

Leadership development, whether through a specific programme or mentoring and coaching, for example, is seen as important in education so that we build and develop a pipeline of skilled, prepared leaders. Yet my research has shown that BME female leaders in secondary education in England face several barriers that are related to both their gender and ethnicity, which can be hard to separate.

What is evident is that many of the enablers of success that female BME leaders highlighted are the result of individual factors rather than enablers within the system itself. Systemic barriers exist that make it difficult for there to be a uniform pipeline of future leaders. For BME female leaders, instead there is a kinked hosepipe, which – due to the kinks and splits in several places causing leaks – loses considerably talented teachers who could be potential leaders. An effective talent pipeline for female BME leaders simply does not exist yet in education. Those who do succeed do so purely on individual terms rather than the system nurturing, valuing and facilitating their progress into leadership. We still have a long way to go in order to achieve this goal.

How then can organisations support, develop and retain BME women as leaders in education? A McKinsey report has been examining diversity in the workplace for several years and its research highlights the benefits of diversity for businesses. Its conclusion is stark:

companies in the top quartile for gender or racial and ethnic diversity are more likely to have financial returns above their national industry medians. Companies in the bottom quartile in these dimensions are statistically less likely to achieve above-average returns. (Hunt et al., 2015)

If we replace 'companies' with 'schools', and 'financial returns' with 'student progress', does that help our organisations to take a harder look at recruiting and retaining BME women leaders?

The impact of #WomenEd led to the development of other grassroots organisations, including @BAMEedNetwork (#BAMEed), @LGBTedUK and @DisabilityEd_UK. They all promote a vision of diverse leaders and leadership and offer a range of practical strategies to increase leadership diversity for individuals and organisations.

- Put up posters about these groups in rooms where staff collect so they can connect with people who will support them
- Publicly publish statistics on the breakdown of staff according to ethnicity and gender at each level of the organisation to compare with your student population
- Publish the gender and ethnic pay gap each year and share with employees and governors/trustees
- Develop recruitment and selection strategies that actively seek to increase the numbers of BME applicants, including stating your commitment to diverse leadership in job advertisements
- Ensure all individuals involved in recruitment are aware of legal requirements and the duty of equality and understand what is meant by unconscious bias
- Support your BME staff with informal and formal opportunities to be mentored and coached. Consider partnership arrangements with other organisations if needed to achieve this
- Take advantage of #TeachMeets, #LeadMeets, other events and conferences (and unconferences for #WomenEd) to enable #BME women leaders to connect with role models who are succeeding as leaders
- Review the diversity of those on your governing/trustee board and think through ways to ensure a diverse group

Anoara Mughal (@anoara_a), writing on the BAMEed website, sums up why we need to challenge ourselves more to bring about the changes needed:

Not only will the children from ethnic backgrounds benefit by having more BAME positive role models but so will the children native to this land. Imagine a land without prejudice or hatred but filled with tolerance, patience and understanding. (Mughal, n.d.)

CHANGING THE SYSTEM

- How diverse is the leadership team of your school, multi-academy trust (MAT) and the local authority? How representative is this of your local pupil population?

- Why do you think it is important to have diversity in leadership in schools and what are the benefits of having a diverse leadership team in your educational organisation?
- What do your female BME colleagues say would support them to be senior leaders?
- What actions should be taken at an individual, organisational and systemic level?
- What good practice have you noted, and could this be transferred to other educational organisations?

ROLE MODEL: FATIMA AL-FAHIRI

I found out about Fatima Al-Fahiri about a decade ago and her achievements just blew my mind away. My first reaction was to wonder why I hadn't heard about her and why weren't pupils taught about her in schools? The answer to the latter was probably because she was female and a Muslim and our curriculum in schools only rarely acknowledges the contributions of those who are not male and white.

Fatima al-Fahiri came from a prestigious and wealthy family. She was a young, forward-thinking, educated woman, indeed a visionary, who decided to use her wealth for the greater good. In the year 859, she founded the oldest academic degree granting university that still functions today, the stunningly beautiful University of Al-Qarawiyyin in Fez, Morocco. This became one of the world's leading spiritual and educational institutions. That's quite a legacy for learning, which truly demolishes the myths that sadly still exist about Muslim women today.

Her family originally migrated to Qayrawan (also spelt Kairouan in modern day Tunisia) and this lent its name to the mosque. The library at the university has recently undergone extensive restoration and reopened to the public in May 2016. The library's collection of over 4,000 manuscripts includes a ninth-century Qur'an and the earliest collection of hadiths (collection of the sayings of the Prophet Muhammad PBUH). Notably, the university predates both Oxford and Cambridge by 300 years.

Students travelled there from all over the world to study Islamic studies, astronomy, languages and sciences at the university and many distinguished thinkers such as Abul-Abbas, the jurist Muhammad al-Fasi, and Leo Africanus, the famous author and traveller, studied there. There are many other prominent names associated with the institution including the jurist Ibn al-Arab, the historian Ibn Khaldun, and the astronomer al-Bitruji (Alpetragius). Non-Muslims were also welcomed and were amongst its scholars, including Gerber of Auvergne who went on to became Pope Sylvester II. He is attributed as introducing Arabic numerals and the concept of zero to medieval Europe. One of the university's most famous students was the Jewish physician and philosopher Maimonides.

Photo Al-Karaouine University (Al-Qarawiyyin) in the city of Fez, Morocco (Anderson sady/CC-BY-SA-3.0)

REFERENCES

Bush, T., Glover, D., Sood, K., Cardno, C., Moloi, K., Potgeiter, G., and Tangie, K. (2005) *Black and Minority Ethnic Leaders*. Nottingham: National College for the Leadership of Schools and Children's Services.

Coleman, M. (2005) *Gender and Headship in the 21st Century*. Nottingham: NCSL.

Coleman, M. (2007) 'Gender and educational leadership in England: A comparison of secondary headteachers' views over time', *School Leadership & Management*, 27(4): 383–399.

Crenshaw, K. (1989) *Demarginalizing the Intersection of Race and Sex: A Black Feminist Critique of Antidiscrimination Doctrine, Feminist Theory and Antiracist Politics*. Available at: https://philpapers.org/archive/CREDTI.pdf (accessed 18 July 2018).

Department for Education (DfE) (2016) *Schools, Pupils and their Characteristics: January 2016*. Available at: https://assets.publishing.service.gov.uk/government/uploads/system/uploads/attachment_data/file/552342/SFR20_2016_Main_Text.pdf (accessed 17 October 2018).

Fuller, K. (2017) 'Women secondary head teachers in England: Where are they now?', *Management in Education*, *31*(2): 54–68.

Garner, R. (2015) 'Headteachers urged to recruit more black and ethnic minority teachers', *The Independent*, 5 April [Online]. Available at: www.independent.co.uk/news/education/education-news/headteachers-urged-to-recruit-more-black-and-ethnic-minority-teachers-10157044.html (accessed 17 July 2018).

Gunaratnam, Y. (2003) *Researching 'Race' and Ethnicity: Methods, Knowledge and Power*. London: Sage.

Haque, Z. (2017) *Visible Minorities, Invisible Teachers: BME Teachers in the Education System in England*, The Runnymede Trust and NASUWT. Available at: www.runnymedetrust.org/uploads/Runnymede%20ReportNEW.pdf (accessed 18 July 2018).

Haque, Z. and Elliott, S. (2017) *Barriers: Visible and Invisible Barriers: The Impact of Racism on BME Teachers*, The Runnymede Trust and the NUT. Available at: www.teachers.org.uk/sites/default/files2014/barriers-report.pdf (accessed 18 July 2018).

Haynes, N. (2016) 'Being a headteacher as a BME woman', *Ambition School Leadership blog*, 6 January [Online]. Available at: www.ambitionschoolleadership.org.uk/blog/finding-courage-reach-headship-bme-woman/ (accessed 17 July 2018).

Hunt, V., Layton, D. and Prince, S. (2015) *Why Diversity Matters*, McKinsey Report, January [Online]. Available at: www.mckinsey.com/business-functions/organization/our-insights/why-diversity-matters (accessed 18 July 2018).

Loden, M. (1978) Conference Speech cited in '100 Women: "Why I invented the glass ceiling phrase"', *BBC News*, 13 December [Online]. Available at: www.bbc.co.uk/news/world-42026266 (accessed 18 July 2018).

Lynch, S. and Worth, J. (2017) *Keeping Your Head: NFER Analysis of Headteacher Retention*, NFER Research Report, April.

McNamara, O., Howson, J., Gunter, H. and Fryers, A. (2008) *No Job for a Woman? The Impact of Gender on School Leadership*. Birmingham: NASUWT.

McNamara, O., Howson, J., Gunter, H. and Fryers, A. (2010) *The Leadership Aspirations and Careers of Black and Minority Ethnic Teachers*. Birmingham: NASUWT/NCSL.

Mughal, A. (n.d.) *BAMEed Network* [Online]. Available at: https://www.bameednetwork.com/ (accessed 18 July 2018).

Osler, A. (1997) *The Education and Careers of Black Teachers*. Buckingham: Open University Press.

Page, D. (2015) 'The visibility and invisibility of performance management in schools', *British Educational Research Journal*, *41*(6): 1031–1049.

6

DOING LEADERSHIP DIFFERENTLY

ANGELA BROWNE

KEY POINTS

This chapter will:

- Consider the role that unconscious bias and discrimination have had in creating opportunities for women to do leadership differently

- Consider the ways in which women leaders have evolved their leadership to suit the needs of an organisation

- Consider leadership approaches typically assigned to men and women and the validity of these assignations

- Highlight the value of authentic leadership and decision-making that arises when women choose to do leadership differently

INTRODUCTION

Differences are not intended to separate, to alienate. We are different precisely in order to realise our need of one another.

Desmond Tutu, 2016

Through a series of case studies this chapter will explore the ways in which four women committed to doing leadership differently. It will illuminate the path on which many women find themselves, a path strewn with obstacles of unconscious bias and possibly discrimination and prejudice, and will consider the way in which walking that path leads to a commitment to do leadership differently. I will explore the assimilation of leadership styles that many women leaders adopt to overcome assumptions about women's behaviour as leaders, and show how increasing confidence can lead to the ultimate decision to work differently, allowing an authentic, confident leader to arise and bring about change.

BREAKING THROUGH THE GLASS CEILING

For many women, working within a patriarchal system has meant the need to find ways of dealing with unconscious bias and even prejudice and discrimination. To break through the glass ceiling and take on what have been traditionally male roles or leadership positions, women are often punished for failing to embody stereotypically assigned feminine behaviours or for embodying these same behaviours. Cikara and Fiske (2009) argue: 'Women must walk a narrow path: their competence may be doubted as women, but their warmth may be doubted, as professional women. These two dimensions operate differently making it difficult for professional women to gain respect for their competence and liking for their warmth at the same time' (2009: 79).

In the conclusion of their article they argue that it is almost an expectation that women substitute warmth for competence and vice versa because there is a belief women can't be both. This false dichotomy assumed between competence and warmth is central to the mission articulated by the role model headteachers in this chapter who have all used elements of both to do leadership differently.

There are so many issues that affect women's progress into leadership roles. The decision about whether many women are given the chance to lead, let alone do leadership differently, is one that is intercepted along the way by selection panels that bring their biases to the table. Dee-Ann Schwanke (2013) argues that organisational structures, including 'male dominated "old boys' networks'", increase ambiguity about advancement. She draws attention to the likely 'homogenous and longstanding' nature of some of these networks as well as the reticence of men to welcome women into them.

This phenomenon chimes with Claire Cuthbert's experience of applying for headship. Claire grew up in the North-east of England and applied for her first headship in County Durham, an area with which she was familiar and a school where she knew she could make a difference. Yet at the end of the selection process she fell foul of the biases that may be seen with all male selection panels and male-dominated candidate groups. The outcome led her to commit to doing things differently when she did find herself in an influential position to support the progression of women leaders.

CASE STUDY: CLAIRE-MARIE CUTHBERT

Claire-Marie Cuthbert is the CEO of The Evolve Trust. She has over 15 years of leadership experience in some of the country's most challenging schools including both primary and secondary contexts.

My leadership journey began from very humble beginnings on a council estate in the North East of England. I am one of four siblings and was the first person in my family to go to university. I went into education, as I wanted to open doors for young people especially those from disadvantaged backgrounds.

I started my teaching career on Teesside, also in the North East of England, became an Advanced Skills Teacher early on in my career and progressed through the traditional head of department, head of faculty route into leadership. It wasn't until I joined the Future Leaders Programme in 2010 that I entered senior leadership and moved to one of the most challenging schools in the country where just 12% of children achieved 5A*-C grades (not including English and Maths) and with over 500 fixed term exclusions.

I stayed there for a few years and the school was transformed, celebrating record results with 45% of children now achieving 5A*-C grades including English and Maths and education making a real difference to children and the community. However, the time had come for me to apply for my first headship and to spread my educational wings.

After extensive research I applied for a job, still in the North East of England in County Durham where I felt I could make the most difference. The day of the interview came. I had done all my research, had had a mock interview, practised interview techniques till the cows came home, but what I wasn't prepared for was an all-male field and an entirely male interview panel. The other candidates were of a similar age, late 40s-50s, and they were all dressed in grey pin-striped suits. I felt I had clearly misjudged things as I was the youngest by 20 years! I tried incredibly hard to make small talk but wasn't at home with their discussions about football or golf.

To my surprise, I did make it to the final two candidates. I knew that if I was not successful I would learn and grow from the feedback and be better prepared for any headship interview the next time. But then the feedback came. They said I was an outstanding candidate, given my age (although I have no idea why they commented on my age which they knew when they selected me for interview!). Apparently, I excelled in the teaching and learning tasks and demonstrated passion and enthusiasm to serve children from disadvantaged communities. That said, they believed that the local mining community would be more aligned to a male figure head than that of a female one and, on that basis, I had been unsuccessful. And there, in that feedback, my headship dreams were crushed. I was bitterly disappointed, not because I didn't get the job, but because there was nothing I could do to improve for next time. It was several years before I reapplied for headship as my confidence was seriously knocked. I did go on to become a very successful head and then an executive head of a federation of schools and now a CEO.

That experience taught me how not to do things! It also taught me that I am more resilient than I initially thought. As a leader, I am passionately committed to developing future leaders and ensure that feedback that is given is always developmental. Since becoming a Head and a CEO I have also become obsessed with the interview panel and making sure that interviewers are representative of the demographic we serve. As a Trust we have adopted blind recruitment strategies to alleviate any unconscious bias that may exist.

DOING LEADERSHIP STYLES DIFFERENTLY

Women's experiences of leading are often stories of leading differently because the fact that they have made it to a position of leadership often means they have had to do something differently, had to stand out in some way to enable it. It has been argued that women lead in very different ways than men. Kuhn and Villeval (2015) found that women tended towards a more collaborative and less individualistic style of working. Writing in *The Conversation*, Psychology Professor Alice Eagly (2016) explains,

meta-analyses, have found that female leaders, on average, are somewhat more likely to be democratic, collaborative and participative than their male counterparts – that is, they invite input from others and attempt to build consensus. Men, in contrast, are more likely to be autocratic and directive in their approach.

And yet in the Catalyst study *Women 'Take Care', Men 'Take Charge'* (2005), what emerged was that the belief that men and women lead differently, which persists in the modern day workplace, is rooted in gender stereotypes, not necessarily in reality. Indeed, this study emphasises that the perceptions of our workforce are altered by virtue of people's biases, expectations and perceptions of how men and women lead them.

If we accept that preconceptions about gender roles influence judgements about male and female leaders, it is easier to understand why there is an assumption that many men will favour a more directive or authoritative style of leadership and that many women prefer affiliative or coaching styles. We are products of what is expected of us, of our own and others' assumptions and biases. Eagly and Johannesen-Schmidt (2001) argue that we 'occupy roles defined by [our] specific position in a hierarchy but also simultaneously function under the constraints of [our] gender roles' (2001: 783). Literature on leadership has tended towards definitions of styles that are primarily agentic or primarily communal. Eagly and Johannesen-Schmidt (2001) say distinctions are made between task-oriented styles and interpersonally oriented styles of leadership. However, during the 1990s a body of research began to emerge suggesting that leadership approaches to which women might tend (or be expected to tend) allowed for more transformation in the workplace. Indeed, several studies cite women as being much better suited to a transformational leadership style, a style in which, through 'mentoring and empowering followers, such leaders encourage them to develop their full potential and thereby contribute more capably to their organization' (Eagly and Johannesen-Schimdt, 2001: 787).

Transformational leadership incorporates inspiration, positivity for the future, individualised consideration of others, as well as contingent reward, which makes it a rich derivative of aspects of both agentic and communal styles. With this in mind, doing leadership differently (especially in challenging circumstances) could be seen as consciously adopting a transformational style in order to achieve the maximum impact and to accommodate the transformation and the changing needs of a school as it improves.

When Alison Kriel took up post at her school she committed to exactly this, shifting and strategically implementing different leadership approaches as and when they were needed. She was not one leader suited to one school, but an evolving leader suited to the evolution of her setting. The clarity with which she set out on her leadership journey, as well as the detail of the journey itself, encapsulates the #WomenEd values of clarity, collaboration, challenge and change.

CASE STUDY: ALISON KRIEL

Alison Kriel is an experienced headteacher who has worked in several schools, led two schools and transformed a failing London school in the bottom 1% of schools to a highly successful school in the top 0.1%.

> When I first took on a failing school, my biggest challenge was there was no leadership. The school had limped with erratic leadership for some time. There was a lack of systems and each person worked in the best way that they could. Every class was different and the teachers, who were clearly worn down by lack of leadership, felt isolated and overwhelmed.
>
> I needed to sort things out quickly. Strategy and systems needed to be put into place. I did not have a leadership team and teaching was

dated and uninspired. That in turn led to pupil disengagement and most teachers seemed to be containing challenging pupil behaviour rather than teaching. I used a model of instructional leadership, as there were no other options at that stage. It is a lonely way to lead, and soul destroying.

Things changed as the school embraced the systems and strategies I introduced, and we began to see stronger pockets of teaching excellence and better learner outcomes. I also started to develop a strong, collaborative, leadership team. Trust, transparency and mutual respect were our guiding principles. I created opportunities for collaborative leadership of the school and began to develop a sense of shared responsibility and ownership.

Each person within the team had clear roles within the school. By setting up a model of collaborative leadership, I could ensure we all had time to do those roles effectively. Our system was simple. At the start of the year we set a rota on who led the day-to-day running of the school each day. It was equally distributed, even counting to ensure we had equal numbers of Fridays and Mondays. I had an equal share. The person on duty that day made all the decisions and knew that I was available if they felt overwhelmed or uncertain about anything. I remained accountable for all decisions, but they knew that I would support them in any way that I could and that I had their backs.

As the leadership team became more collaborative and purposeful, we moved towards a model of distributed leadership. We became solution focused and disciplined. Mutual respect was strong, and we valued our similarities and differences, seeing them as a necessity for being a balanced team.

We spent a huge amount of time together. We wanted to make a difference together and recognised that no one person was the keeper of knowledge and information. We therefore undertook learning walks, observations, recruitment, book scrutinies. Data analysis was in small groups and shared with the team. It meant that all decisions in relation to school improvement were informed decisions and there was shared understanding on rationale behind all decisions. Discussions in the school were at a deeper level and much less anecdotal. We had meaningful conversations about strengths and areas for development. We were not drawn into trying out new fads and we were much more solution

(Continued)

(Continued)

focused in deciding what was best for our school, often adapting methods to make it bespoke to our needs – 'our school's way'.

I always took overall responsibility for the school. If it failed, I failed. However, I took pride in the fact that I was part of a leadership team that took it upon themselves to have a shared responsibility for performance, attainment and the growth of the school, meaning the success of the school was not built around the success of one leader. We moved to a model of embedded, sustainable success.

Distributed leadership gave me more time to be available to the whole staff as well as to the pupils. My meetings with teachers were less about feedback and more about what they saw as areas of development for themselves, what they needed from the school to grow and who could help them. They knew that it was not my responsibility to make them into great teachers. The responsibility was theirs but they could draw on my support and that of the whole leadership team.

The model of distributed leadership cascaded through the school. Teachers at all levels of the profession supported each other and teaching assistants took on increased responsibilities by co-leading in and out of the classroom. It enabled us to have a staff team that was truly diverse at all levels which in turn had a significant impact on pupil outcomes.

LEADING DIFFERENTLY WITH AUTHENTICITY

Regardless of the means that many women leaders take to reach the top positions in education, and whatever leadership style they adopt when they get there, what soon became clear for the role models that follow is that the approach to leadership that brings success won't necessarily keep you there. Perhaps this is why Alison's journey, from lonely directive leader through to passionate collaborative leader, is so powerful, and perhaps this is the answer to Claire's success at moving from the leader of one school to the successful CEO of many. For both women there was a realisation that the strategies and leadership style they needed in order to secure a post needed to change to enable a more authentic version of themselves to emerge.

At some point, for the women leaders in this chapter, what becomes evident is that the need for deepening levels of authenticity is a fundamental dimension to doing leadership differently. And so beyond the leadership style or the initial approach adopted by our next two contributors lay the discovery of who they were and who they wanted to be as leaders.

For Rachael, the journey towards greater authenticity in her leadership role marks the difference between her approach to leaders and those of others. As she so rightly says, the difference arises simply through Rachael being herself!

CASE STUDY: RACHAEL SHAW

Rachael is the Headteacher of Branston Junior Academy in Lincolnshire, East Midlands.

I've worked with leaders who can definitely be classed as "authoritarian", who sashay about the establishment, full of their own importance, throwing out rules, regulations and orders in a seemingly never-ending fashion. I've also worked for leaders who come across as very "laissez-faire", not wanting to get involved in any real decision-making for fear of upsetting others. Obviously, neither of these extremes, in my humble opinion, are useful for leading a group of people to achieve success.

Having recently completed my MEd, with a dissertation looking at different leadership styles, I have submerged myself in the different varieties. Coaching, democratic, facilitative, transactional, transformational and visionary are just a few that can be brought up with a simple search of the internet. But each one, I feel, would be too restrictive if one were to simply use only one style of leadership for every situation that occurs. Surely the successful leader has a tool-kit of leadership styles to use when dealing with the different situations and different personalities that we engage with each day? Just like an effective teacher who doesn't use just one way of teaching a subject, surely an effective leader has to assess the situation and take the time to get to know the individual(s) concerned? Then, consideration must be given to the desired outcome for the person, the situation and the leader before deciding how best to deal with it all.

In my research for my MEd dissertation, I came to the conclusion that the most effective way to be a leader was to be an "authentic" one. Curry (2000) states, 'we need to move away from formulaic descriptions of leadership, towards understanding the contexts within which we are working, thus enabling greater "self-exploration" (2000: 21). Thompson (2016) believes that effective leaders need to develop an understanding of the 'complexities of human experience'. He states that they should believe in a 'conception of human existence [that is] fluid and dynamic, with each of us challenged [and] taking ownership of our actions' (2016: 29). Lawler and Ashman (2012) state that leaders should rely less on 'traditional modes of control' and develop 'true empowerment', when everyone is involved in an 'inter-personal

(Continued)

(Continued)

engagement – not ignoring but acknowledging and negotiating power asymmetries' (2012: 340). Indeed, many other eminent people in the world of educational leadership have similar opinions to mine, that the most effective leader is one who is trying to get the best out of their team, not necessarily the most.

However, my approach to leadership has taken time to develop. Time for me to get to know each individual and try to understand their viewpoints. Time to consider how I can help each staff member to continue to develop. Time to think before reacting to a situation, balancing individual staff development with the needs of the specific situation and the most beneficial end goal for all concerned. But above all else, time to self-reflect, to celebrate my successes, work on my weaknesses, always considering why something was or was not effective and being prepared to show others my vulnerabilities. I believe that an effective leader is one who is authentic: they can share their triumphs without sounding pompous, they can admit when they have made a mistake and they can say when they don't know the answer. In essence, they are human and realise they need the people around them.

The confidence that Rachael Shaw demonstrates in becoming the leader she wanted to become, is echoed in Teresa Roche's account of her journey. Teresa also demonstrates that when we break out of the conventions of what is expected and do leadership differently, there are possibilities to create a sustainable and visionary educational system for the future.

CASE STUDY: TERESA ROCHE – LEADING DIFFERENTLY WITH CONFIDENCE

Teresa Roche is Headteacher at Dronfield Henry Fanshawe School in Derbyshire, which is located in the East Midlands of England.

Our philosophy is one in which commitment is valued and celebrated. This goes back over 18 years to the time when I was taking up my first headship and thinking about the lessons I had learned about leadership along the way. What would I have wanted as a young NQT, then a middle and senior leader? What had caused me to question things that had happened along the way in two different schools prior to becoming a Deputy Head in my third? I was then one of very few women involved in senior leadership positions at that point in the school due to its nature and history rather than any bias but over time that situation changed. I remember questioning the situation of women leaders back in 1992 when the thought of #WomenEd or any other group bringing together female leaders was non-existent. I am so glad that we now have this global community who can share their knowledge and understanding and help others to develop the skills required to move into leadership positions and play their part in ensuring equality of opportunity for all.

Transparency, integrity, care and trust are hugely important in any relationship and the same applies to schools. They are hard won and easily lost if the trust of those you are leading disappears. They help to develop synergy across the school community, which empowers all involved be they students, staff, parents, carers, governors or members of the local community. It takes time and effort to promote these values actively in every area of the organisation. Great communication is key and then effective self-evaluation; it will fail if leaders believe that there are no glass walls or ceilings in their school but those who work there and contribute greatly to its success experience it differently.

I do feel there are leaders who expect compliance in many aspects of our work as leaders. This may be due to the pressure of external accountability which can lead to a rigid, authoritative way of leading. To me, managing a school based on compliance alone leads to a culture where people are constrained. There is an invisible checklist which can inhibit growth and, when things do go wrong, there is a blame mentality. It also leads us to a situation where there is a feeling of "I'm doing everything asked of me, it is for someone else to do this, that or the other and it's not for me to stick my neck out". Leading a school where commitment is valued, however, leads to a culture that permeates the school. Such a culture creates a strong community where every person matters and through which opportunity is offered at all levels irrespective of the gender, status, ethnicity, sexuality or any other characteristic of the people concerned. This may be particularly important for those staff who are less confident of their own possibilities and so don't necessarily seek out opportunities for growth.

(Continued)

(Continued)

We introduced an associate programme, which affords any member of staff the chance to associate to a role in school and to try it out before deciding if it might be for them. It also fits with #WomenEd's mantra to be 10% braver! Support and teaching staff can take up these opportunities to give them confidence as they move forward in their careers. Recently we have set up an area of our website where staff, particularly those who may be away from school for an extended period such as maternity or shared parental leave, can join in and still feel a part of our day-to-day work as well as having a forum to share thoughts and concerns with those who are further down the line in their career. We still have plans to look at a crèche facility as we believe this would be hugely beneficial for staff in terms of wellbeing. It is an important commitment as leaders to assist as much as we can in the growth of others.

What the contributors to this chapter have in common is that they have all shown a commitment to doing leadership differently. They have done it differently by breaking through the glass ceiling to ensure that the conditions for other women leaders improve, by clinging on to the glass cliff and adapting a leadership style to bring a school and its community back from the brink, by committing to authentic leadership over any particular textbook style or by confidently changing the system through trusting in people rather than seeking compliance. Their accounts are shining examples of the #WomenEd values in action.

DOING LEADERSHIP DIFFERENTLY IN ORGANISATIONS

For some organisations, embracing 'doing leadership differently' requires a huge culture shift. We work in times of high stakes accountability and stepping away from traditional methods of school leadership requires bravery and faith. Yet from governance through to the teacher in the classroom there are opportunities to be courageous and to lead in ways that diverge from the status quo. Both Claire Cuthbert and Teresa Roche implemented organisational change in setting up aspects of school life. Claire's 'obsession' with interview panels and selection processes enables the school to ensure that opportunities to demonstrate unconscious bias or discrimination are actively negated as part of the process. In Teresa's school, plans to provide a crèche facility anticipate potential for schools to offer a greater degree of support to the workforce, particularly to women.

Leaders at all levels in school can take steps to address the assumptions that the community in the school may well have formed regarding the way in which men and women lead differently and the suitability, therefore, of a man on a woman to a particular post. And there are opportunities to consider when to do leadership differently, what style of leadership may be suited to the school to accommodate the particular phase of the school, and to seek to test this out in potential candidates.

The radical notion for organisations is to consider the extent to which narratives about leadership styles, questions about leadership in interviews and tasks that test out the competency of candidates can be set aside in favour of assessment activities that enable potential appointees to articulate with authenticity the difference they can make and the value they can bring as individuals to a school community. This is demonstrated in the way that Hannah Wilson (2017), then one of #WomenEd's five national leaders, designed a recruitment process for a brand-new school: 'Our tasks were designed around candidates demonstrating their values. We were not trying to catch anyone out, we were trying to allow them all to shine.'

For the leaders in this chapter, the freedom to lead authentically is doing leadership differently. And to lead as a woman, according to the wealth of research in all the chapters in this book, appears to centre around the value of relationships and community, as Alyse Nelson describes: 'Women have been forced to operate from outside closed networks, which means they've had to adapt by creating their own worlds; they've learned to unite peripheral, disenfranchised communities into collectively organized and governed microcosms' (2012).

She could be describing #WomenEd! Nelson also highlights that 'People want to be considered, to belong, and to contribute'. Harnessing such a desire to contribute and the opportunity to embrace authenticity in leadership is a search and an invitation that all organisations can commit to, and in so doing, wholeheartedly embrace doing leadership differently.

CHANGING THE SYSTEM

- How do you enable your leaders and governors/trustees to be aware of the issues of unconscious bias and discrimination?
- How can you plan and design your recruitment process differently to enable assessment to be unencumbered by gender bias?
- How do you recognise the phase the school is in with enough clarity to inform decisions about the leadership approaches needed?
- What does it take to commit courageously to transformational approaches to leadership?

REFERENCES

Catalyst (2005) *Women 'Take Care', Men 'Take Charge': Stereotyping of US Business Leaders Exposed*, Knowledge Centre, October [Online]. Available at: www.catalyst.org/knowledge/women-take-care-men-take-charge-stereotyping-us-business-leaders-exposed (accessed 18 July 2018).

Cikara, M. and Fiske, S.T. (2009) 'Warmth, competence, and ambivalent sexism: Vertical assault and collateral damage', in M. Barreto, M.K. Ryan and M.T. Schmitt (eds), *The Glass Ceiling in the 21st Century: Understanding Barriers to Gender Equality*, Psychology of Women Book Series (pp. 73–96). Washington, DC: American Psychological Association.

Curry, B. (2000) *Women in Power: Pathways to Leadership in Education*. New York: Teachers College Press.

Desmond Tutu Peace Foundation (2016) *Ten Pieces of Wisdom from Desmond Tutu to Inspire Change Makers in 2016* [Online]. Available at: www.tutufoundationusa.org/2016/01/03/ten-quotes-from-desmond-tutu-to-inspire-change-makers-in-2016/ (accessed 18 July 2018).

Eagly, A. (2016) 'What does social science say about how a female president might lead?', *The Conversation. com*, August. Available at: http://theconversation.com/what-does-social-science-say-about-how-a-female-president-might-lead-61255 (accessed 5 June 2018).

Eagly, A.H. and Johannesen-Schmidt, M.C. (2001) 'The leadership styles of women and men', *Journal of Social Issues*, *57*(4): 781–797.

Kuhn, P. and Villeval, M. (2015) 'Are women more attracted to cooperation than men?', *Economic Journal*, *125*(582): 115–140.

Lawler, J. and Ashman, I. (2012) 'Theorizing leadership authenticity: A Sartrean perspective', *Leadership*, *8*(4): 327–344.

Nelson, A. (2012) 'How women lead differently, and why it matters', *Fast Company*, 9 August [Online]. Available at: www.fastcompany.com/3000249/how-women-lead-differently-and-why-it-matters (accessed 18 July 2018).

Schwanke, D. (2013) 'Barriers for women to positions of power: How societal and corporate structures, perceptions of leadership and discrimination restrict women's advancement to authority', *Earth Common Journal*, *3*(2): 15–28.

Thompson, N. (2016) *The Authentic Leader*. London: Macmillan Education.

Wilson, H. (2017) 'Calling all flamingos', *The Hopeful Headteacher blog*, 18 December [Online]. Available at: https://thehopefulheadteacher.blog/2017/12/18/calling-all-flamingos-join-our-aureus-family/ (accessed 18 July 2018).

7

REMOVING THE BLINKERS

CLAIRE NICHOLLS

KEY POINTS

This chapter will:

- Explore what can be learnt from combining leadership in different contexts

- Reflect on the reasons why certain leadership experiences are valued more than others

- Consider how leading in different sectors means you can bring far more than transferable skills to any role

- Suggest why and how school leaders should see those with varied experience as an asset

INTRODUCTION

When someone asks me what I do, I proudly say I'm a teacher. The word instantly conjures up an image in people's minds of what I do day-to-day. They picture me sitting reading a story to toddlers or standing in front of a class of teenagers. They're keen to know what I teach. I'll usually focus on one part of my job, explaining that I'm a SENDCo (Special Educational Needs and Disabilities Coordinator). Then comes the question that I used to dread: 'Primary or secondary?' It seems so simple, so innocuous and you'd be forgiven for wondering why I don't just say I currently work in a secondary school. Often though, I inhale. 'Well . . .' I begin, before launching into an explanation that I never feel does my role, or my experience, justice. For those whose jobs don't fit neatly into the narrow expectations of most people's idea of a teacher, this is a constant struggle. Sometimes it's a mere frustration, but some days it feels like we don't fit and we can begin questioning ourselves and wondering: Do I teach too little? Am I actually a leader? Is my work valued?

Connecting with the #WomenEd community has allowed me to answer these questions with confidence and clarity. I've learnt to embrace my unique position, understanding that it is the very things that I used to question that make me an effective leader. I now see my career as a deliberate, cohesive choice rather than a series of disparate experiences. There are common threads running through my work, my volunteering and my activism. Community, challenging the status quo and collaborating with others are essential to my work. Career paths don't have to be straight lines and I've learnt that mine owes less to chance than I previously assumed. It is logical that my focus on authenticity, my passion for inclusion and my determination have led me here. This is not luck or a happy accident, but a reflection of my skills, knowledge and values.

MY LEADERSHIP JOURNEY

I came to teaching after accidentally realising I was good at it. A summer job with a language school showed me that teaching was the destination I was searching for. I was nearing the end of a law degree that I knew would no longer be my chosen career. Whilst law wasn't for me, those hours in the classroom left me energised and excited. An initial teacher training course at Master's level satisfied my academic leanings and I qualified as a primary school teacher with a specialism in French, a far cry from my role now.

Sometimes, you take on a role in order to find out that it isn't for you. One year as a languages coordinator was enough to convince me to turn down the possibility of teaching GSCE French later in my career, and by then I had already discovered my vocation. Inclusion is my passion and I've pursued this, starting with a small responsibility within the department, through a whole school middle leadership role and a long-term secondment to the senior leadership team of a special school. In September 2018, I moved to a new school to lead inclusion and run a specialist resource base. On my journey to my current role, I've realised that it's perfectly fine to start your career without any clarity around where you're heading. Exploring different avenues will give you the confidence to know when you've found the right one.

Early in my career, I began to embrace identities that may seem incompatible. I combined my growing leadership role in school with taking an active part in my trade union – in school, locally and nationally. Far from being at odds with school leadership, my role in the union taught me to collaborate with those who hold different views from me, balance support and challenge, communicate clearly for a range of audiences and plan for change – all skills that have helped me to develop as a school leader. I've also been a staff governor for several years and have worked with pupils aged 3 to 19. These experiences suggest an image of a climbing wall to leadership rather than the traditional ladder, and have led me to understand that there is more commonality across the educational sector than many think; human resources, finance, pedagogy and leadership are not unique to any one setting. Unfortunately, I have also learned that not all experience is equally valued.

THE HIERARCHY OF SECTORS

Binary divisions seem entrenched in education. Special and mainstream; primary and secondary; academies and local authority schools; state and private; leadership and classroom teachers. We're all defined by where we work and sometimes the gulf between us can seem impossible to traverse. Switching between sectors is something we're told only to do if we're sure, because getting back is next to impossible. Mintz et al. stated that 'we know anecdotally that when teachers enter special education, it is fairly rare for them to go back to mainstream' (2015: 108). Moving from mainstream schools to special schools, however, is a common move, perhaps because all teachers will have trained in mainstream schools. When I trained in 2008, the choice was between primary and secondary. Ten years later, this is still the case. Whilst new routes of entry into teaching are appearing all the time, there is still no dedicated specialist education qualification; even those completing school-based training in a special school are required to complete a placement in mainstream. This speaks volumes. What part of mainstream education is essential to teaching, yet absent in a special school? Coupled with the absence of the special sector from much of the discourse about education, this sends a clear message about how much it is valued.

It could be argued that special schools simply feature less as there are fewer of them. They make up less than 5% of state-funded schools. If it is simply a numbers game, then the current educational landscape would arguably look different. There are just over 3,400 state-funded secondary schools compared with close to 16,800 state-funded primaries (DfE, 2017). It doesn't feel, however, that the primary sector dominates.

Given that the early years sector is arguably even lower within this perceived hierarchy, you could be forgiven for thinking that it's a case of student age and qualifications. This hypothesis only works, however, if you ignore the existence of the further education sector. It often feels like our oldest students, and those teaching them, are frequently left out of the discussion unless they're based in a secondary school. So what is going on? Why do Twitter, #TeachMeets, conferences and training not reflect the balance of schools and teachers? Even average salaries lag behind in primary schools (DfE, 2016: 7). With far more primary school teachers out there, surely they should be our profession's loudest voice? I fear it's partly to do with gender.

Whilst women make up the majority of teachers across all sectors, there are relatively more men in secondary schools. The school workforce data shows that 63% of secondary teachers are women, compared with 85% in primary (DfE, 2016: 7). Could it be that men are more likely to be voluble, to present their work, share their research and celebrate their success? Does our profession assign more worth to traits that are traditionally associated with men?

#WomenEd are challenging this stereotype and giving women the confidence to speak up, but the problem is more subtle and pernicious than there being lots of female primary teachers who don't speak out. Regardless of the actual gender balance of the teachers in each sector, primary (especially early years) and special school teaching are seen more as caring professions, and care is a highly gendered topic. The perceived hierarchy of pre-16 education seems to place secondary education on a pedestal, ahead of primary, early years, and finally special education. As the role of a teacher in each sector involves more caring and nurturing, this teaching and learning experience is valued less when applying for other roles. It's important to note that when I mention 'caring', I'm not implying that secondary school teachers don't care about their students. I'm using caring as shorthand for physical contact, support with toileting and personal hygiene, and the teaching of skills such as eating – the skills which are traditionally associated with motherhood, and therefore women.

Having and using these skills does not preclude one from being an excellent teacher, with secure subject knowledge and solid behaviour management skills. In a study of teachers who had moved from mainstream to special school teaching, Lewis found that '[n]one of the teachers in the study felt that it was inappropriate or devaluing of their professional expertise for them to play a role in the care needs of the students in their classes' (2014: 188). These skills are not exclusive to specialist settings; many pupils have some level of care need and I've encountered all of the examples above in mainstream, albeit at a lower frequency.

I wonder though, whether these tasks would make it onto a job application of someone looking to move into mainstream. I've certainly never seen feminine coded words such as 'compassionate', 'warm' and 'kind' (Gaucher et al., 2011: 125) on a person specification.

Whilst I wouldn't go as far as to argue that other sectors think special and primary education are an easy choice, it's clear that a mainstream secondary school teacher will be seen to have more relevant experience when interviewing for a special school leadership post than if the situation were reversed. Whilst a personal statement or covering letter may highlight experience of leading whole school initiatives, managing budgets and holding staff to account, skills that can be applied to a multitude of situations, relevant experience is still very much sector based, with some sectors seen as easier to transfer from than others. So how do you make the jump?

TEACHING

When applying for a role in a different sector, the advice is to focus on so-called 'transferable skills'. My experience across the sectors, however, has taught me that I don't have separate expertise which I selectively apply, depending on the context. I am a skilled teacher and leader and can do my job well in a variety of contexts. Excellent teaching is not sector-specific. I have taught every year group, from terrifying afternoons covering a nursery teachers' planning, preparation and assessment (PPA) time to teaching young adults with disabilities about relationships and consent. Whilst the content and language differ greatly, the basic aspects of a lesson never change: know your pupils, find out what they already know, teach them what they don't and make sure they've understood. I'm not claiming that I could teach every lesson. I recently tried to support a Year 11 student with their biology revision and it seems I've forgotten everything I knew at 16! We undoubtedly need teachers with good subject knowledge in our secondary schools. If this is the key concern on appointment though, why are there such high numbers of teachers who teach outside of their subject area? The Department for Education Workforce Census shows that 80% of those teaching engineering don't have a relevant post-A-level qualification in the subject. The same is true for half of those teaching Information and Computer Technologies and 37% in physics. In humanities, this is also a common phenomenon; a quarter of those teaching history did not study it at graduate level. Even in the core subjects of English and Maths, there are non-specialists (18% and 22% respectively) (DfE, 2016: Table 12). If we're prepared to be flexible about subject qualifications, why not age-related experience?

Children don't change so rapidly at age 11 that they need a completely different school experience after the summer holidays at the end of Year 6. If I were a headteacher, I think I'd favour a primary languages coordinator over a religious studies teacher for a Spanish post. It seems we are prioritising experience with a particular age of pupil over all else. This isn't the only way though and it's up to those of us who have experienced the value of collaboration to communicate this more widely.

When comparing the experiences of those who had moved into special schools, Lewis' interviewees 'were clear that there were not significant differences between mainstream and special education' (2014: 186) and this confirms my experience working across the two sectors; we have far more in common than divides us. If confidence is a barrier due to certain skills honed in special or early years education being perceived as softer, or more feminine, then those of us who have challenged these biases need to speak up. By continuing to communicate our values as we move into leadership, we can reach a wider audience.

LEADERSHIP

When recruiting to senior leadership teams, I'd argue that this focus on sector-specific experience is even more pronounced. Gay describes how lower pay scales and less chances to experience other sectors 'subliminally devalue the contribution of primary leaders and reduce the desire for leaders to move across the key stages' (2017). Given the reduction in teaching time that often comes with promotion, this seems nonsensical. Understanding the context of those you're leading is essential. An effective leader, however, doesn't need to know more than every-one they lead. I can tell whether a geography lesson is being well taught, and combined with input from a subject specialist, I can support a teacher to get the best out of their pupils. With teachers coming from a wide range of higher education disciplines, leaders are regularly line managing and supporting outside of their subject area. I've been observed teaching languages by a senior leader with a physical education background, and maths by a former Religious Studies teacher, and nobody questioned their ability to make an informed judgement, so why not extend this to working across different phases?

Leadership skills are universal and 'commutable' (Gay, 2017). I'd go as far as to argue that the higher you go, the more generalised the skills used. Reflect on the conversations you've had as a leader, or with senior leaders in schools: How many are truly ones who you feel wouldn't transfer to another sector or phase? Consider those around child protection, staffing and budgets. How often have you been asked your opinion on data that isn't from your class, or given a colleague advice on a difficult conversation? These things aren't phase- or sector-specific. Interview can-didates are often given tasks with information about pupils they've never met, scenarios they haven't encountered and data that doesn't even exist. So why don't we trust experience gained in other sectors more? There have been various initiatives to encourage those outside teaching into the profession, so surely there are benefits about moving phases?

DIVERSITY OF THOUGHT

It's safe to stick with what we know. Even if anonymising applications reduces unconscious bias on the basis of gender, class or race, leaders are able to pick people just like them: the same university, training provider or qualification; a key phrase in a personal statement which evokes a particular style of teaching; familiar job titles, predictable career paths and stability of sector. Even at a time when it's unusual to remain with one employer for many years and person speci-fications count experience in more than one school as desirable, alarm bells still ring if we can't see consistency. If we use familiarity as an appointment tool though, where do the new ideas come from? How do we innovate if we work with people who all have the same experiences as us? Instead of appointing on the basis of working in the same phase of education, you could seek out those with shared values and the same ethos, who may bring skills your organisation needs. As an individual, consider widening your job search; an organisation that suits you may be somewhere you hadn't previously considered. Have the confidence to communicate what you could add.

When I moved from teaching primary- to secondary-aged pupils, my practice didn't change in a substantial way. I was able to suggest some ways of working which my new colleagues adopted, as well as incorporating their successes into my lessons. Likewise, when I started in a special school, I was able to make improvements quickly by replicating a system of data tracking that had been useful in mainstream. Understanding how to track pupils' achievements if they are working well below age-related expectations has been something I've brought back with me to mainstream. It's not unusual to learn from colleagues, or from other schools, but I'm arguing that we shouldn't limit this to passing on tips at #TeachMeets; let's encourage staff from other sectors to join our schools and make a difference. The connections we make can translate into real change if we challenge ourselves to work as a community, rather than as isolated teachers.

A related issue is the nature of the areas in which leaders become experts. We don't have data as to how many women lead SEND or pastoral roles, nor do we know how many men do the timetable in a secondary school or lead numeracy or mathematics. We are sure that physics specialists are mostly men. Who leads on the curriculum in your school? Who leads the early years team or sorts out the behaviour of unruly students at the end of lunchtime? Which gender leads the smallest schools and which leads the largest schools or largest MATs? We don't have the data, yet I'm sure that we all have similar answers to these questions. Perceptions about gender that may influence such choices are shared in Chapters 3 and 6. Here I ask you to consider gaining experience in an area that is outside of your comfort zone. Timetabling should be as much about meeting needs and priorities as it is filling slots and hierarchies of subjects. And as software can now do much of the heavy lifting in creating a timetable, the human dimension is very important and is where women stereotypically triumph. If women are excellent in building teams, why aren't they leading the largest schools and MATs? Diversity of thought is important in deciding who is tapped on the shoulder when new opportunities arise and who asks to gain new skills.

COLLABORATION IS KEY

Despite my desire to encourage staff to move between sectors, I'm not advocating parachuting in an expert. Nobody can have a significant impact on school improvement on their own, and relying on one person certainly wouldn't bring about the diversity of thought that I'm calling for. Mintz et al. describe the importance of expertise being shared to increase capacity rather than concentrating skills and knowledge in one person. The 'risk that other teachers see SEND and inclusion as something which is not their job, cannot be understated' (2015: 30).

This is a real danger with most areas of expertise. If we see a single person as solely responsible, then the danger is that everyone else stops caring. Leadership roles are more specialised and there are fewer of each role the higher you go. Given that Gaucher et al. coded the words 'communal', 'responsive' and 'together' as feminine, compared to the masculine 'independent' (2011: 125), are fewer women opting for senior leadership as they see it as a less collaborative environment? The other danger of working in isolation is that it leaves no room for succession planning. If you're the only person who understands a particular area, then what happens when you leave? In a worldwide climate of increasingly difficult recruitment, schools can't take it for granted that a specialist in your area will replace you, so you need to leave some knowledge and skills behind. That's an excellent argument for building a diverse team who will work on the timetable, for example, or in the early years.

Collaboration is one way to solve this issue. If staff are exposed to a wide range of views, diverse ideas and ways of working, then they can broaden their own practice. By learning from those in other sectors, they can widen their scope even further. This can be done in a variety of ways: school visits, secondments, teacher exchanges. With most schools within partnerships in one way or another, through the local authority, multi-academy trusts, cooperatives or federations, this should be easy to achieve.

FINDING MY VOICE

I've been lucky enough to have worked in primary, secondary, special and mainstream. I've worked with people who I consider to be experts, whether they're newly qualified teachers or people who've been in the job for decades. I have been shaped by all these professional encounters and so it is collaboration which has enabled me to become the teacher I am today, with clear strengths in several areas, but with enough flexibility to adapt and learn. Consider your own career: What are the experiences you've enjoyed the most? Is there anything you've left behind because you felt that it wasn't compatible with your current role? It might not be too late to find space for it.

When thinking about my career, with the help of #WomenEd I've achieved the confidence and clarity I need to be able to articulate why my path through teaching has taken the shape it has. Not necessarily expected, not always smooth, but with a thread that binds all my experience together. For me, my roles are about championing equality: supporting those who need an advocate, as a colleague, trade union representative, governor and SENDCo. I chose leadership to make more of a difference for those who need it. With clarity about your values, seek out experiences that will enrich you as a professional; seek out role models who will give you the confidence you need to make a change.

REMOVING THE BLINKERS IN ORGANISATIONS

It's clear that we have a recruitment and retention crisis in education. Worth et al. state that the 'proportion of working-age teachers leaving the profession each year has risen steadily between 2010 and 2015' (2017: 4). Many teachers are advised to try a different school before leaving education altogether, but this isn't always the answer. For me, my unhappiness as a primary teacher wasn't down to my school. It was that I wanted to focus on a different part of education, and by facilitating this, my school kept a teacher who otherwise may have left the profession. Communication was key here; if I hadn't been confident enough to discuss my waning enthusiasm for my role honestly, my headteacher may never have suggested a change. I would always advocate this approach. If you never ask, you'll often be left wondering what may have been. My situation was unusual though; there aren't many schools where you can change jobs so readily. Whilst you can communicate your career wishes as an individual, we need to do more as a profession to effect change.

OPENING UP THE JOBS MARKET

Schools are finding it increasingly difficult to recruit staff. It's not uncommon to hear school leaders state that there were only applicants who did not have the relevant experience or expertise for a post. Whilst recognising that there are some minimum expectations, especially for subject knowledge in secondary roles, leaders should consider whether they're being too quick to reject on the basis of sector-specific experience. Why not employ a primary teacher and timetable them to add value to Key Stage 3? Why not welcome a special school teacher into a primary vacancy, acknowledging that they'll have extensive knowledge of developing early literacy and numeracy skills? If we can foster an increased acceptance of diverse experience, we can open up the jobs market and retain teachers. I owe a huge amount of my confidence as a leader to the women who have supported my career over the past decade, even though I wasn't exactly what they were expecting. Seek out role models, and if you suspect you are one, remember how much of an impact your words can have on those who look up to you. As women leaders, we need to provide other women in the profession with a community they can turn to for support.

FLEXIBLE WORKPLACE STRUCTURES AND CHALLENGING HIERARCHIES

Alongside the drive to increase flexible and part-time work opportunities within education, we need to look at the structures within organisations and see where there is room for change. By offering staff secondments or short-term leadership opportunities, organisations can develop talented leaders and create clear succession plans. This should be much easier with the number of teachers now working within multi-academy trusts, but it doesn't seem to be happening. Worth et al. stated that '[t]here appears to be little evidence to date that MATs are better able to retain teachers by providing opportunities to move within their structure' (2017: 6). If even within multi-academy trusts, staff are not being given new positions, roles and challenges, then the vast majority of teachers only experience working in another environment when they change jobs.

As well as challenging the perceived hierarchy of sectors described earlier in the chapter, it's time to be radical about challenging the hierarchy within schools. If you're in a position of leadership, challenge those staff who dismiss others' experiences as not valid enough. Question whether your recruitment processes really are fair, or whether by specifying a certain type of experience, you're unintentionally creating a senior leadership team who are homogenous in some way.

If organisations have been brave enough to open up their vacancies to those with varied experience, then they've got a talented workforce with diverse skills; schools should use that expertise. If there is nobody on the senior leadership team with experience of working in a special school, ask a class teacher without leadership responsibilities how best to include disabled pupils. In a special school, consider giving the leadership of assessment to someone who has extensive experience of tracking, monitoring and moderation that comes with mainstream teaching. A former Year 6 teacher would be able to lead curriculum for Year 7 far more effectively than someone who has been teaching Key Stage 4 for the past decade. We need to be bold if we're going to effect change.

CHANGING THE SYSTEM

- Do you bring all of your experience and expertise to work? If not, why not?
- How can you work with colleagues in other sectors to share expertise, develop the skills of your teachers and deliver the best possible experience to your pupils?

- How are you making it clear that you value experience from other sectors, attracting a wider range of candidates to your vacancies?
- Are you giving your staff the opportunity to communicate and collaborate with those in other sectors to maximise retention?

ROLE MODEL: RUBY TANDOH

It may seem strange for a teacher to choose a food writer who appeared on *The Great British Bake Off* as a professional role model, but Ruby Tandoh is someone I greatly admire. She embodies the #WomenEd values and demonstrates a commitment to authenticity across her work. Whilst appearing on the BBC's baking show, she was criticised for showing too much emotion. An ITV's *Loose Women* declaration of 'never cry at work!' (ITV, 2016) was thankfully met with a discussion of the double standards of women crying being seen as manipulative, but it's just one of the ways in which Tandoh supports women to be themselves. Since becoming well known through her television appearance, she has used her platform to communicate her clear messages about 'food, pop culture, art and queerness' (Tandoh, 2018a) and has resisted any urge to surrender to mainstream popularity by diluting her message. Instead, she states that '*Flavour*, though less commercial than *Crumb* and less "successful" by some barometers, is actually the thing I'm most proud of in my entire life. . . . I feel like I've finally found my voice' (Haynes, 2016). This reflects the confidence and clarity I've found around my professional self since becoming part of the #WomenEd movement. She has spoken openly about her eating disorder, and is vocal about challenging the mainstream food and dieting industries, most recently in her book *Eat Up!* where she partners recommendations for further reading with the advice that '. . . each of these voices is interested in one particular facet of morality, and their approach might not always align with what's feasible or desirable for you' (Tandoh, 2018b: 211). This is one of the things I love most about Tandoh. In an industry based on telling people what and how to eat, she advocates doing what's right for you.

REFERENCES

Department for Education (DfE) (2016) *Schools Workforce in England 2010 to 2015: Trends and Geographical Comparisons*. London: DfE.

Department for Education (DfE) (2017) *Schools, Pupils and their Characteristics: January 2017*. London: DfE.

Gaucher, D., Friesen, J. and Kay, A.C. (2011) 'Evidence that gendered wording in job advertisements exists and sustains gender inequality', *Journal of Personality and Social Psychology*, 101(1): 109–128.

Gay, A. (2017) 'We must mend the primary and secondary split in education leadership', *Schools Week*, 14 January [Online]. Available at: https://schoolsweek.co.uk/we-must-mend-the-primary-and-secondary-split-in-education-leadership/ (accessed 17 May 2018).

Haynes, S. (2016) 'Gal-Dem in conversation with Ruby Tandoh', *Gal-Dem*, 16 October [Online]. Available at: www.gal-dem.com/gal-dem-in-conversation-with-ruby-tandoh/ (accessed 27 March 2018).

ITV (2016) 'GBBO's Ruby Tandoh crying on the show', *Loose Women*, 23 September [Online video]. Available at: www.youtube.com/watch?v=6WTfwpnmLFk (accessed 27 March 2018).

Lewis, D. (2014) 'The experience of moving from mainstream to special school: a case study of eight teacher's transformative learning', Ed.D. thesis, Canterbury Christ Church University.

Mintz, J., Mulholland, M. and Peacey, N. (2015) *Towards a New Reality for Teacher Education for SEND – DfE SEND in ITT Project Report and Roadmap for SEND*. London: UCL Institute of Education.

Tandoh, R. (2018a) 'Hi', *Ruby Tandoh* [Online]. Available at: https://rubytandoh.com/ (accessed 27 March 2018).

Tandoh, R. (2018b) *Eat Up!* London: Serpent's Tail.

Worth, J., De Lazzari, G. and Hillary, J. (2017) *Teacher Retention and Turnover Research: Interim Report*. Slough: NFER.

8

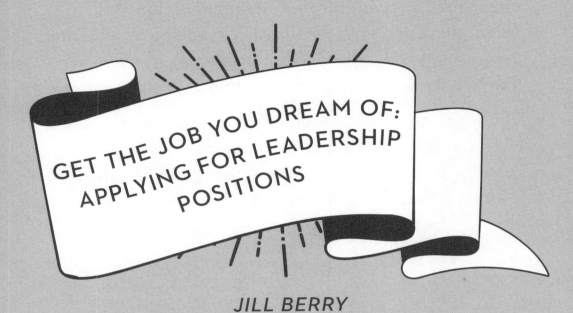

GET THE JOB YOU DREAM OF: APPLYING FOR LEADERSHIP POSITIONS

JILL BERRY

KEY POINTS

This chapter will:

- Explore the process of applying for leadership positions at all levels in education settings, from your first promoted post to headship, and from your initial response to the advertisement for the position to managing your transition into the role

- Encourage you to reflect on how you can be discriminating and select an appropriate vacancy that will allow you to fulfil your potential and become the leader you wish to be

- Offer advice as to how you can increase your chances of success through the application and selection procedure: writing a compelling application; performing well at interview; preparing to make a positive beginning in your new role

- Show how the eight #WomenEd values are relevant to the process of stepping up to a new level of responsibility and the expanded sphere of professional influence that this will offer you

INTRODUCTION

This chapter focuses on your leadership journey, potentially through middle leadership, senior leadership and into headship. Whether you are a serving or aspiring leader at any level, it should help you to consider where you are going in your career and how you can get there. How can you give yourself the best possible chance of success through the application process? How can you convince the selection panel (and perhaps yourself) that you have what it takes to embrace a new professional identity and step up to the next level of responsibility?

Begin by considering what type of role is the next most appropriate professional challenge for you, and what kind of educational context will suit you best. For example, what phase and sector are you considering – a primary, secondary or all-through school, a college, alternative provision, maintained or independent, UK or overseas? You need to feel that the time is right: you are committed and enthusiastic about expanding your sphere of professional influence and accepting a new challenge. You have to select a role in an educational setting that you believe is suited to you and in which you can develop into the leader you hope to be.

Consider how you can draft a compelling written application that will secure you an interview and give you the opportunity to meet face-to-face those who will be making the appointment decision. How can you prepare yourself, and conduct yourself, so that your interview performance is strong and you clearly demonstrate that you are a good match for this role in this context?

Finally, if you are successful in the selection process, what can you do in advance of formally taking up the role to ensure you give yourself the best possible chance of making a positive beginning in your new post? How can you manage the transition into your new professional position as effectively as possible?

FINDING YOUR FIT

I often say that not getting a new job might not be the worst thing that could happen to you. Getting the *wrong* job could be.

Whenever you apply for a new role, you need to see this as a two-way process. There are a number of things you undoubtedly feel you will gain, should you be successful – if not, then why would you apply? You may be looking for a fresh challenge, for a new and interesting professional context, for increased responsibility which will expand your professional sphere of influence and enable you to make a greater difference to the lives of more people. However, you should also consider what you have to offer. What do you bring to the role, the team you will lead, the organisation you will work within? How are your skills and qualities a good fit for this particular post, in this institution, at this time?

When you are preparing to apply for a leadership position, internal or external to the organisation where you are currently employed, you need to feel that there is a synergy between what you are looking for and what they are looking for. Successful application, and, in fact, successful performance once in post, depend on there being a good match between the two. Is this a role that will enable you to fulfil your professional potential? If you take on a leadership role within this specific institution at this stage, will it enable you to be the kind of leader you dream of being? Is there a coherence in terms of the ethos of this educational establishment and your own vision and values – your educational philosophy and your commitment to leading in a way that you consider is true to who you are and what you believe? Do you have the transferable skills, and the temperament, to do this job and to do it well – recognising that you will continue to learn and grow in post? No one does the job perfectly from day one – in fact, perfection is something that none of us ever achieves.

If, on reflection, your answer to these is clearly 'no', then my strong advice would be to think again, look elsewhere and perhaps wait a while. There is no 'right time' to move, so resist the impulse to apply because your peers appear to be moving on, or others suggest you should. If those who lead you express confidence in your capacity to move up, this should bolster your confidence, but you need to feel that the time, the school and the role are the right fit for you.

CRAFTING THE WRITTEN APPLICATION

If the research you have done into the role and the organisation convinces you that this is the right next step for you, and that this is a context that will enable you to achieve what you hope to, then the first challenge is to ensure your written application is compelling and convincing. Of course, if you fail to do this, you have no opportunity to impress at interview.

Look carefully at the information you have been able to amass so far, including the documentation they have sent you about the post and the organisation. Ask yourself what they seem to be looking for in the successful appointee, both in terms of what they explicitly say, but also with respect to what they seem to imply. Go beyond the information supplied by the institution itself and look carefully at anything else that might help you work out what capacity there is for an incoming leader at this level to make an impact. The most recent inspection report, for example, should complement what they themselves have actually said. Use what you can find on the web and any information that comes to you from others who know the school (though be circumspect about this, recognising that others' views will be subjective and not impartial). Visit the school if you can: this is essential if applying for headship. Use all the information you can gather to establish what they appear to need from the incoming leader.

Then demonstrate, as clearly and powerfully as you can, how you fit the bill. Connect what they *need* to what you could *bring* to the position. Show your suitability, using your past achievements and experiences to exemplify and support what you claim. Focus on the impact you have had in the past, the skills you have developed and the potential you have. But keep bringing it back to this specific context, the job description and the person specification. Start from where *they* are and not where *you* are, and do not simply supply a list of everything you have done in the past and expect the selection team to make the connections for you. Ensure you are positive, assertive and confident in the language you use.

Ask someone whose judgement you trust to read your application and to give you honest feedback. It has to be completely accurate, logically structured, clear and persuasive. Sometimes when you have lived with an application for some time you find you begin to lose your objectivity, so asking someone else to read it can help you to spot ways in which you can correct and improve it before you send it off. My blog about applications is a useful aide memoire (Berry, 2017). If you are applying for headship you will be interviewed by a majority of governors, which is a different experience. Vivienne Porritt (2017) has written a very useful blog to support such an application.

PREPARING FOR AND PERFORMING WELL AT INTERVIEW

So if you are sure that this is a fit and you are a match for what they need, and you have spent time, thought and care on a strong written application, you very much hope that you will then have the opportunity to convince them further at interview. All the preparation you have done so far, and the careful consideration you have given to this role, and to your suitability for it, will serve you well as you prepare for the next step.

My advice to those preparing for interview is to go through all the information again with a fine-toothed comb, and your own application, and consider what *you* might ask, were you a member of this selection panel. Consider the interviewers' point of view:

- If you were trying to assess the suitability of a range of candidates, what might you want to ask them? Look at the job description and the person specification.
- What do you need to probe in order to evaluate the relative strength of the different contenders for the post?
- How will the interview offer you the opportunity to judge whether those you meet are capable of doing this job, and doing the job well?
- Will they bring valuable skills that complement the skills of those with whom they will be working? How do you gauge their leadership capacity?

Once you have generated a list of potential questions from the perspective of the interviewer, then consider how you would respond as the candidate. What could you say to ensure you answered the question directly and succinctly? What examples could you draw on to add weight to your response? How do you keep on track, focus on what is relevant and most compelling, and impress the panel with your positive qualities and – importantly – your capacity to continue to develop and strengthen once in post and given the right balance of challenge and support?

And practise these responses. If the first time you say the words you have thought about saying is in the interview itself, you have missed an opportunity. Ask someone to direct the questions at you so that you can try out what you might say (and crucially, how you will round off the answer and move on. Avoid rambling!). If possible, can they think of follow-up questions to direct at you that you haven't anticipated, to test you further? And in the interview itself, of course, be very careful to listen attentively and answer the question you have actually been asked, rather than the similar question you may have anticipated.

In addition to the formal panel interview you may well be asked to give a presentation – prepare it carefully, practise in front of someone supportive and astute and ask them for feedback, and, if you have a time limit, be very careful to stick to it. It may help your confidence to draft out what you will say in the presentation, but please do not read to your audience. Rehearse, and then make brief notes so that you can *speak* to them instead – with confident eye contact, a degree of spontaneity and a natural manner. If you use a PowerPoint presentation, for example, keep it concise and simple, and always have a Plan B in case the technology lets you down.

If you are also faced with practical tasks, be aware that this is something that is difficult to predict and specifically to prepare for. Such tasks will test your judgement, your capacity to think quickly and to act appropriately and perhaps your capacity to express yourself and make decisions under pressure. This can be both terrifying and exhilarating! But if the selectors are committed to finding out who is the best fit for what they need, and whether this is the right post for you, such activities can prove invaluable.

DEALING WITH FAILURE AND SUCCESS

There may be several stages of the selection process depending on the leadership level for which you are being considered, but ultimately, the process will be completed and (subject to satisfactory references and other checks of suitability) a decision will be made.

If you are successful, you will no doubt feel elated and energised. This may in time be mixed with feelings of apprehensiveness and trepidation – now you have to *do* the job! You will need to manage the news of your success and, if this is an internal promotion, there may be other issues to contend with: Were there other, unsuccessful internal candidates with whom you will continue to work, and so have to navigate a potentially sensitive relationship? As you step up to your new level of responsibility, how can you negotiate the change in your professional persona, and your relationships across the whole school, while still being true to yourself? If this is an external appointment, how can you ensure that your current professional community recognises that you are still committed to doing your present job to the very best of your ability, and that excitement about your future move will not be a distraction that dilutes your professional effectiveness? How do you balance dealing with the present while planning for the future?

If you are unsuccessful and disappointed, that is something you will have to manage carefully. If you believe that you did justice to your past achievements, current talents and future potential, it may be easier to accept that on this occasion you were not successful and move on. Perhaps, despite your conviction that you were a good match to the role, other candidates were even better suited: we never know the strength of the field within which we are judged. Perhaps the selection panel did not fully appreciate what you had to offer, despite your best efforts and, if this were the case, would you really want to work with them?

If you feel retrospectively disgruntled with your own performance and *do not* feel that you did justice to your capabilities, that can be frustrating, especially if this was a job you badly wanted. However, it is important that you recognise what you learnt from the experience and how you can use this in future to increase your chances of success when applying for other jobs. My advice is to be quite systematic about this. Make a list of what you think you did well and would repeat. What do you think you should perhaps have done differently, or in addition? Why? How can you use this learning for future benefit?

Always ask for specific feedback from the organisation to which you have unsuccessfully applied. Be respectful, polite, professional – never be aggressive or rude about this, however bruised you may feel. Antagonising one prospective employer may well have negative repercussions with respect to future posts, and it is an inappropriate way to respond to disappointment in any case. Let it go . . . Sometimes institutions are reluctant to give any feedback at all and some may give you a bland, unhelpful response (Would you *really* want to work with them if this were the case?), but others may well give you constructive feedback that does inform your future steps. Again, be thorough and methodical here. Make a list of points to remember and pull them out when you prepare to go through the application process elsewhere.

MANAGING THE TRANSITION INTO THE ROLE POSITIVELY

If you are successful in the appointment process, you enter into what I call the 'lead-in' period – that crucial time between getting a job and formally stepping into the role. There are some circumstances where incoming leaders are 'catapulted' into their new position, rather than being led into it, and if this is the case then clearly you have to get on with it! But for most of us, several months may elapse between 'getting the badge' and 'sitting in the chair'. This is an important time that is not without its challenges, but which, if effectively managed, can help you to accomplish a significant amount.

You will, no doubt, continue to do a demanding job in your current role, and this is important. You do not want those you work with at this time to consider you less committed or effective because you are starting to be preoccupied with what is to come. You will recognise that your current employer is paying you to do your current role until the end of the notice period, and they deserve your diligence and consideration.

However, there may be additional demands on your time with respect to preparing for the role you are about to step into, and you will need to negotiate a careful balance between the two. There are ways in which you can ready yourself for the new challenge, and in starting to understand more fully what lies ahead, to meet people and to consolidate your learning, while at the same time colleagues (and perhaps others, especially at headship level – parents, prospective parents, students, governors, and members of the wider community) begin to get to know you. It is a time for you to start to 'know and be known'.

So you will need to consider how to allocate your time, and find the mental space to focus on doing a good job now while preparing to do a good job in the future. It is a worthwhile use of your time to do some systematic planning here and to look at the 'lead-in' period in its entirety, give careful thought to what you hope to achieve and how to go about it. Talk to the head of the new school, or the chair of governors if you are moving to headship, about their expectations, and talk to your current head to seek their advice. How can you navigate the challenge of the lead-in period to best effect while ensuring you protect your own wellbeing and achieve a sustainable balance between your personal and professional responsibilities and commitments?

Ask yourself what you need to do now, and what can wait. What actually *needs* to wait until you are properly in post, getting to know the legacy you are stepping into and the people with whom and through whom you will work to make your aspirations a reality? You may well have a vision for what you wish to achieve in your new post but remember you cannot impose a vision on others. You will need to work positively alongside them so that you move towards a clearly understood, corporate vision to which they have subscribed and to which they have an emotional engagement. A new leader puts their own stamp on this vision, but you cannot import a pre-conceived, pre-planned vision into a new context and expect all to go swimmingly. You rely on others to work alongside you to bring the best ideas to fruition (and not all the best ideas will come from you). Do not alienate or terrify them before you can even get started on this.

You will have much to think about as you manoeuvre your way through the lead-in period. It is an exciting, energising time, but it is also demanding. Listen, learn, use sound judgement, pace yourself. A well-planned and executed lead-in period can smooth your transition into a new role and ensure you make the most positive beginning when you are officially in post. I wish you well in your journey.

THE RELEVANCE OF #WOMENED'S CORE VALUES

Throughout the process of applying for a new leadership role, the 8 Cs, #WomenEd's core values, will be crucial.

You will need *clarity* as you investigate and decide upon the right role, in the right establishment, at the right time (for you and for them) – clear thinking, and a clear and compelling strategy throughout the application and appointment process.

Your *communication* skills, both written and oral, will definitely be tested as you present a convincing argument that you are not only a suitable person for the post, but you are actually the MOST suitable candidate they will see.

You will need to make a persuasive case to show the *connection* between what you have to offer and what the selectors appear to be looking for – and what the school needs – from its incoming leader. You will also start to make a connection with the school community you plan to join. This begins from your first email, or telephone call, or visit, and is strengthened throughout the application and interview process.

All of this requires *confidence* – confidence without arrogance or complacency. You are still learning, you know you do not have all the answers and, to a degree, although you can prepare in a number of ways, you will ultimately learn the job from doing the job. You need to have confidence in your capacity to do so.

There will be many opportunities for *collaboration*, and this will be key during the lead-in period when you begin to develop the relationships that will enable you to be effective in your new leadership role, and to find it fulfilling and rewarding.

You will be part of a new *community* – even if this is an internal promotion, you may be joining a different leadership group, such as the heads of department/middle leaders, or the senior leadership team, to which you will make a positive contribution and from whom you will learn and receive support.

There will be a fruitful and stimulating *challenge*, through the appointment process, during the lead-in period and once you step into the role. This will test you, and rising to the challenge will help you to strengthen and grow. When the challenge seems tough, remember 'rough seas make the best sailors'!

And your new leadership position will enable you to achieve positive *change*, to move things forward, to make an even greater difference to the lives of children and adults, and to realise, over time, your vision as an educator and a leader. In my view, successful leadership relies on strong relationships and effective communication. It also relies on the action you take and the change you effect.

ORGANISATIONAL PERSPECTIVES

With respect to different organisations and their approach to the issue of applications for leadership roles, it is clearly crucial that they are open and transparent, avoid gendered language in advertisements, interviews and when giving feedback (Tickle, 2018), be clear about what they want when they are making their appointments while still being open-minded, treating all candidates fairly, being alert to and avoiding bias, and managing the process positively and efficiently. Chapters 6 and 11 give further advice on improving the application process to better support female applicants, and Chapter 11 also gives advice on negotiating salaries or flexible working.

Every unsuccessful candidate is a potential ambassador for your institution: you want those who are disappointed to feel regretful that they did not succeed on this occasion but to recognise, and to communicate to others beyond the organisation, that they were well treated and the process was organised, fair and respectful. This includes giving constructive feedback to disappointed candidates. And please let applicants go home whilst your panel deliberates. The practice of candidates waiting together in the staff room should be dead and buried!

All educational institutions have to accept that they have a responsibility to support the professional development of all their staff and to do all in their power to help these staff fulfil their potential and achieve success. This will involve supporting professional development at all levels, perhaps investing in coaching and mentoring to help colleagues recognise what they may be capable of in the future and to aspire to becoming their professional best and, when talented individuals do apply to move on, being positive, constructive and encouraging, even while we may well be sorry to see them leave. Can organisations offer both emotional and practical support, such as feedback on draft letters of application, and practice interviews?

CHANGING THE SYSTEM

If we change ourselves, we change the system. The leaders appointed today will be the ones who are appointing the leaders of tomorrow. We can aim for a virtuous circle as we all invest in making the very best of our human resources in schools and other educational establishments so that the adults fulfil their potential and, in so doing, support and challenge the students to fulfil theirs.

In the light of what you have read in this chapter, consider the following:

- What research do you need to do now to identify the most appropriate next step in your leadership journey? Set out some parameters to help you decide what are non-negotiables for you, in terms of the next role you will apply for, and where you are prepared to be flexible.
- Identify where you can access support through the application process. Who should you talk to, or perhaps shadow? Who could you ask to read a rough draft of your application?
- Consider how you will prepare for interview and whether there is anyone who would be prepared to give you a practice interview, with follow-up questions, which will enable you to build your confidence and self-assurance.
- If you are unsuccessful, reflect on what you have learnt from the process that will help you with future applications.
- If you are determined to step up to the next leadership position, don't give up! Have faith in your capacity to do this, and in the judgement of those who have confidence in you. It will be worth it.
- If you are successful – take a bow! Now you can use the time in between the offer of the post and your first day to relax and to prepare for your new role.

ROLE MODEL: HELENA MARSH

Helena Marsh is Executive Principal, Linton Village College in Cambridge within the Chilford Hundred Education Trust.

I met Helena when she was Assistant Principal at Sawston Village College. We attended a residential #SLTCamp in 2013, and after that connected through Twitter, met at other spin-off events (including the second #SLTcamp in 2014, which Helena co-organised) and I followed her blog on the social media platform, Staffrm. I thought she was a great example of a strong female senior leader. She moved to be the Deputy Principal at Linton Village College in September 2014.

(Continued)

(Continued)

In 2015, Helena wrote a Staffrm post following her attendance at a conference called 'Empowering Women in Education Leadership'. The post, entitled 'What glass ceiling?', sparked the #WomenEd movement. I responded with a Staffrm post of my own called 'Lost Leaders'. Many other blog posts and discussions followed, Helena and the six co-founders of #WomenEd met to plan the first unconference in October 2015, and the initiative has built from there.

At the time of her early involvement in #WomenEd, the Principal for whom Helena deputised at Linton announced that she was moving on, and Helena was faced with a choice. She was at a relatively early stage of her Deputy Principal career, a young woman with two young children, and the opportunity to step up to the role of Executive Principal (as leadership of the college also brought with it leadership of the small, but growing, Trust) had come along rather earlier than she might have expected. But, as Helena said, if she was espousing the values of #WomenEd, including the exhortation to be 10% braver, she felt that she should challenge any self-doubt, show confidence in her capacity to make the leap, and apply. Her involvement in #WomenEd gave her the courage to do so. She got the job and stepped up in January 2016. Helena has proved herself a courageous, determined, ethical and humane school leader and Trust executive who has integrity, warmth and humour. She is a member of the Headteachers' Roundtable and is starting to exert a wider influence on the world of education beyond her own school and Trust. She is an amazing role model.

REFERENCES

Berry, J. (2017) 'Applying for leadership roles with confidence', reblogged on #WomenEd blog, 5 October [Online]. Available at: https://womenedblog.wordpress.com/2017/10/05/applying-for-leadership-roles-with-confidence/ (accessed 18 July 2018).

Porritt, V. (2017) 'From the Chair – shortlisting', reblogged on #WomenEd blog, 12 October [Online]. Available at: https://womenedblog.wordpress.com/2017/10/12/from-the-chair-shortlisting/ (accessed 18 July 2018).

Tickle, L. (2018) 'Language in school job ads puts women off headteacher roles', *The Guardian*, 19 June [Online]. Available at: www.theguardian.com/education/2018/jun/19/language-school-headteacher-job-ads-puts-women-off (accessed 15 July 2018).

9

THE #HEFORSHE AGENDA: WHAT MALE LEADERS NEED TO DO TO ACTIVELY ENABLE EQUALITY IN EDUCATION

CHRIS HILDREW

KEY POINTS

This chapter will:

- Identify and explore the issues behind the #HeForShe agenda

- Examine the notion that leadership styles are gendered

- Argue that it is the role of male leaders to enable equality in education

- Provide practical strategies that every male leader can employ to promote the #HeForShe Agenda

INTRODUCTION

We work in a profession with a problem. As explored in other chapters, according to Department for Education figures for 2016, 62% of teachers in secondary schools are women, but they comprise just 39% of headteachers, whilst in primary schools, although men make up only 15% of the workforce, they hold 28% of headteacher roles (Department for Education, 2017).

CHECKING MY PRIVILEGE

I am usually in the majority. I joke about how I have the privilege full house: White. Male. English. Straight. Cisgender. Middle Class. I even went to an independent school and the University of Oxford. My privilege gives me advantages. When I speak, people listen. They always have. I expect them to. I've never known any different.

In October 2016 I was invited to the second annual #WomenEd Unconference to speak alongside two of my colleagues from Churchill Academy & Sixth Form about the promotion of gender equality in school leadership. I'd also agreed to take part in a panel discussion on the #HeForShe agenda later in the day. When I arrived, I felt unsettled. Jarlath O'Brien and Jon Chaloner were the only other men there (Vic Goddard joined us later). Looking around the room, I felt like an outsider. Did I belong here?

In the opening session, the #WomenEd steering group asked people to 'popcorn' up to declare what the movement's 10% bravery boost had done for them over the past year. Inspiring and positive examples 'popped' from across the auditorium: women who'd been empowered and energised and invigorated by the pledges they had taken and by the collective permission the movement had given them. Then Jon Chaloner stood up. 'Are men allowed to pop?' he asked. Jon wasn't sure whether he was entitled to speak. He was, like me, in the minority. And because of this, he wasn't sure that his voice 'counted'.

This was my moment of realisation. Jon, Vic, Jarlath and I, as white, male headteachers, go to conferences all the time. We fit right in. We're men in grey suits. The majority. And we speak up without hesitation. What about the female leaders? Have we, in our grey suits and our privilege, unconsciously communicated 'You don't belong here. Your voice doesn't count. You don't have permission to speak?'.

At the #WomenEd Unconference, Jon didn't need permission to speak. We all had permission. We were welcomed. In fact, Hannah Wilson made a point of it, asking our #HeForShe panel 'How do we ensure that men's voices are heard in the #WomenEd community?'. Because #WomenEd is there to redress an imbalance and an injustice, it is explicit in its inclusivity. It makes sure that it is welcoming to all. And it makes sure that everybody has a voice.

I have never consciously excluded anyone from a discussion. But how often have I gone out of my way to make sure that everyone's voice is heard? To make sure that everyone feels welcome? To do what #WomenEd does and make inclusivity explicit? I worry that voices like mine – confident, white, male – can unintentionally intimidate and silence others. I know that reductive, combative, grandstanding voices on social media often do, and of course the same is true in wider society.

Following the unconference, I pledged to amplify and emphasise the message that #WomenEd is an inclusive movement, where men's voices are welcomed to further the cause. But also that, vitally, it is the duty of those with privilege – the white, the straight, the cisgender, the middle classes . . . and, yes, the male – to let everyone know that their voice matters. Irrespective of their background, orientation, ethnicity, identity or gender, they deserve to be heard. And they don't need permission to speak.

BECOMING A #HEFORSHE ADVOCATE

On 20 September 2014, a special event was held at the UN HQ in New York, hosted by Good-will Ambassador Emma Watson, previously best known for playing Hermione Granger in the Harry Potter films. Like millions of others, I watched the speech she gave. I was struck first by her nerves. Her voice quavered and shook as she took in the magnitude of what she was doing. She said:

> You might be thinking who is this Harry Potter girl? And what is she doing up on stage at the UN? It's a good question and trust me, I have been asking myself the same thing. I don't know if I am qualified to be here. All I know is that I care about this problem. And I want to make it better. (Watson, 2014a)

The problem she set out to tackle was the problem of gender inequality, and the campaign she was launching was called #HeForShe. Behind the nerves, there was a steely determination. Even watching it back now, the hairs on the back of my neck stand up. She knew that, in putting her head above the parapet, she was setting herself up for a tidal wave of misogyny. But doing nothing was not an option: she felt duty bound to use her platform to tackle this problem, citing Edmund Burke's maxim: 'All that is needed for the forces of evil to triumph is for enough good men and women to do nothing.'

She told herself firmly, 'If not me, who? If not now, when? . . . Men,' Watson said, 'I would like to take this opportunity to extend your formal invitation. Gender equality is your issue too . . . step forward . . . be seen to speak up . . . be the "he" for "she"' (Watson, 2014b).

The UN campaign was far-reaching and powerful. I signed up immediately because it is important. The campaign asks for a commitment to:

- Express zero tolerance for discrimination and violence against women and girls
- Believe in equal access to social, political and economic opportunities
- Understand that taking a stand for women and girls is taking a stand for humanity
- Speak up when you see physical, emotional or sexual harassment (UN Women, 2016)

These were not difficult commitments for me to make personally, but making them publicly and professionally as a male teacher was a vital part of the process. Being a #HeForShe means making it clear that gender equality is an issue that affects men and women, and that it is male attitudes that need to change for the benefit of both genders. Living the four #HeForShe pledges is a vital part of that process; not being a passive bystander but actively challenging discrimination, taking a stand and speaking up: If not me, then who? If not now, then when? The link to the #WomenEd values of challenge, community and change is self-evident.

As #HeForShe developed, the #BeTheChange strand laid out education-specific approaches that could be taken in support of the movement (UN Women, 2016):

1. *That's not okay.* What does it mean to act 'like a girl' or 'like a man'? Call out gender-biased language from students and teachers alike. Ask the speaker to think about how these comments reinforce gender stereotypes.

2. *No haters.* Online bullies want your silence. Enlist your friends and followers to send messages of support to victims of social media trolling. You'll help turn the internet into a safe space for everyone.

3. *Teach a teacher.* Empower educators to create equality in the classroom. Get the UNESCO *Guide for Gender Equality in Teacher Education: Policy and Practices* (UNESCO, 2015), a step-by-step guide for including gender equality issues in teacher training.

These resources provided and continue to provide a framework for challenging gender inequality in education, particularly in relation to the process of educating young people itself. As teachers, our duty to create equality in the classroom seems widely understood, and the #HeForShe campaign and UNESCO guide were helpful and practical frameworks to help enact this. However, the challenges within the teaching profession needed further work. What could I do, as a #HeForShe school leader, to be a better feminist in ensuring gender equality within my profession?

LEANING IN: LESSONS FROM SHERYL SANDBERG

Sheryl Sandberg's TED talk is entitled 'Why we have too few women leaders' (Sandberg, 2010). The talk, like Emma Watson's at the UN, energised a feminist movement centred on Sandberg's subsequent book (2013) and website: *Lean In* (Lean In, n.d.). Like #HeForShe or #WomenEd, the 'Lean In' movement is inclusive and foregrounds the role of men in developing gender equality (Sandberg, 2015). Despite academisation, there is not always a comfortable fit between all of Sandberg's business-focused advice and the world of school leadership in the UK. I have found the following strategies both thought-provoking and helpful in adapting the Lean In approach to school leadership.

#HEFORSHE STRATEGY 1: MAKE SURE WOMEN'S IDEAS ARE HEARD

Research shows that, in mixed groups, women get less 'air time' than men (Leaper and Ayres, 2007). Men dominate conversations and discussions, both as students in school and as participants in meetings: 'men tend to talk more and make more suggestions, while women are interrupted more, given less credit for their ideas, and have less overall influence' (Lean In, 2018a). Even when they have a seat at the table, cultural gender inequality is so ingrained that the role of women within that forum is diminished. Combating this issue requires all participants to foreground unconscious biases and work hard to break out of traditional roles. This isn't just about women being braver, or bolder, or ensuring that their voices are heard. It is as much about men being aware of the potential problem and ensuring that every participant in meetings and decision-making is given a fair hearing, irrespective of gender.

This process is important not just for gender equality, but also for effective school leadership. If the school leadership team (SLT) consists of eight individuals, but three are making two-thirds of the comments, then that is an ineffective team. All eight need to contribute fully to shoulder the burden evenly and ensure effective decision-making. This relies on each member of the team being up to the task and sufficiently prepared and knowledgeable, but, assuming this is the case, it also relies on a skilful and sensitive chair.

Who chairs your team meetings? Is it always the head or the head of department? One way to ensure equality of representation, whilst also distributing leadership, is to rotate the chair, with explicit expectations of an effective chair. This doesn't just mean managing the agenda and ensuring that the target finish time is met, but managing the discussion so that dominant voices aren't given an undue hearing just because they are the loudest and most confident.

Male leaders in education need to be conscious of being dismissive or refusing to hear what is being said. We need to listen, to engage, and to ensure that everyone gets a fair hearing. Perhaps at your next meeting you could time the contributions of men and women, to see whose voices dominate. There's even an app for that: http://arementalkingtoomuch.com/ or http://www.lookwhostalking.se/.

A good strategy to counteract the male domination of meeting structures is to amplify the contributions of women (Landsbaum, 2016). During meetings, participants repeat and attribute the positive contributions made by women: 'yes, and as Sarah said' or 'that builds on what Leyla was saying earlier'. Equally, colleagues chairing meetings should actively watch out for women being interrupted, and intervene: 'just let Ellen finish, please'. It is also incumbent on leaders to challenge, in private if necessary, repeat interruptors who may not even be aware that they are shutting down contributions to the discussion.

#HEFORSHE STRATEGY 2: CHALLENGE THE LIKEABILITY PENALTY

The second strategy involves challenging perceptions of male and female success. Lean In says: 'When a man is successful, his peers often like him more; when a woman is successful, both men and women often like her less' (Lean In, 2018b). This is not just about promotion within the school, but about the way in which both male and female colleagues perceive female leaders.

School leadership is often about making difficult decisions. When there isn't enough money or time to go around, judgement calls are required to arrive at the best possible (or the least bad) outcome. This is often where unconscious biases can come into play, with the same decision being accepted from male leaders but challenged or undermined from females. Men making the difficult calls and unpopular decisions can be seen as strong, balanced and measured. I have known women's leadership decisions (even if they are exactly the same as the ones I would have made) attributed instead to personal motives, vendettas or hidden agendas. Whereas a man might be seen as confident and assured, women can be seen as aggressive or self-important as though, in some way, they don't belong in that situation making that decision.

The patriarchy sets us all up unconsciously to accept male leadership, as though it's a right; therefore we are more likely to look kindly on decisions made by male leaders, even when they don't go our way. Women leaders, making exactly the same decisions, carry a 'likeability penalty', often resulting in unpopularity, resentment or personal ill-will. It's important that male leaders challenge this likeability penalty, asking colleagues (and yourself) 'would you have the same reaction if a man did the same thing?'. Asking the question picks the scab off the unconscious bias, stopping us in our tracks and forcing us to face up to whether we are upset about the decision, or the person making it.

#HEFORSHE STRATEGY 3:
COACHING AND REVERSE MENTORING

If we are going to address the imbalances and injustices in our education system, then it is vital that we are proactive in our response. Mentoring or coaching aspiring leaders is a positive, helpful step that builds belief, confidence and a 'can do' culture. When first considering this, I was concerned about appearing patronising, or even 'mansplaining' to female colleagues through the process. There is a risk, done badly, that this could be the case: the benevolent patriarch selflessly bestowing his exclusive wisdom and experience on the naïve ingénue. It is not difficult to avoid this situation: follow Wheaton's Law (Wheaton, 2012).

Mentoring and coaching are two different things. Mentoring has a hierarchical structure and is far more likely to lend itself to the patronage model as an expert imparts wisdom and advice to their protégé. I prefer the coaching model, which is non-hierarchical. The coach's goal is to help the person being coached unlock the resolutions to difficulties, or plan their own strategies to overcome challenges, on their own terms and from within their own resources. Being coached allows you to own the changes you are making and developing for yourself, rather than accepting the received wisdom from above. Vic Goddard writes powerfully on this subject. As a new headteacher, he chose to be coached by a junior female colleague (Goddard, 2014). The side-by-side structure removes the risk of reinforcing gender hierarchies.

It is more important now than it has ever been for men to coach and mentor (and to be coached and mentored by) female colleagues. In the wake of the wave of sexual harassment allegations that sparked the #MeToo and #TimesUp campaigns, Lean In reported that the number of male managers who are uncomfortable mentoring women has more than tripled from 5% to 16% (Lean In, 2018c), prompting the organisation to launch the #MentorHer campaign. Although it shouldn't need saying, fear of being accused of sexual harassment should not be a barrier to male leaders mentoring or coaching female colleagues. Wheaton's Law applies again.

Another interesting proposal for flipping the mentoring model is 'reverse mentoring', one of several proposals in the Collaborating with Men project (Stocking and Armstrong, 2016). In this model, a senior male leader is paired with a junior female, but the male mentor is there to learn from the mentee what the organisation is like from a female perspective. Opening up this dialogue enables understanding in the male leader about the issues facing women in the workplace. Any such conversation needs to be rooted in trust, patience and tact, but candour is equally important. The male mentor needs to be open to listening to the female perspective, and prepared to take action to remove barriers, counteract biases and unpick policy and practice that may be perpetuating gender stereotyping or preventing female progression.

#HEFORSHE STRATEGY 4:
CELEBRATE ALL WOMEN'S ACHIEVEMENTS

It should go without saying that it is the role of any leader to celebrate accomplishments and positively reinforce success. As a strategy to encourage women into leadership, it's vital.

Ensuring that successful women are high-profile and visible, and that their achievements are publicised, is a conscious and deliberate technique that can have a significant impact.

When Michelle Obama visited Elizabeth Garrett Anderson School in 2009, she was just getting used to the role of First Lady. Her appearance at the school included her first speech on foreign soil. She chose to talk about gender, and in particular the importance of equal access to education. 'The difference between a struggling family and a healthy one,' she said, 'is often the presence of an empowered woman' (Obama, 2009). This theme would become a touchstone of her time in the White House and beyond. However, the impact on the girls she saw that day was profound, resulting in improvements of almost two grades at GCSE by 2012 (Burgess, 2016a). What Michelle Obama did was personally embody the power of an education, which had taken her from a poor neighbourhood in Chicago to 1600 Pennsylvania Avenue via Princeton and Harvard Law School. As Simon Burgess (2016b) suggests, the overriding message of her appearance that day was, 'I did this; you can too'.

Whilst it is true that we cannot all have Michelle Obama visit our schools to inspire our students (more's the pity), highlighting high-profile successful women's accomplishments can have a transformative impact on students and staff. Are the role models you use in your assemblies male dominated? One of my earliest assemblies as a deputy headteacher featured 'famous failures': The Beatles, Steve Jobs, Walt Disney, Lionel Messi and Michael Jordan. I wouldn't use that assembly now as there are no female role models to be seen. Far better to talk about NASA pioneer Katherine Johnson, Venus and Serena Williams, Laura Trott, Lizzie Yarnold, Sheryl Sandberg, Michelle Obama . . . or any of the countless other female role models out there. Equally, celebrating the achievements of female colleagues in public is vital in ensuring that we do all we can to create a culture of 'she did this; you can too'.

ROLE MODEL: BARACK OBAMA, THE #HEFORSHE PRESIDENT

Barack Obama became the 44th President of the United States on 20 January 2009, and from the outset he embodied #HeForShe leadership. One of his first executive orders, on 11 March of that year, was to create the White House Council on Women and Girls. The first law he passed, the Lily Ledbetter Fair Pay Act, worked to redress the gender pay gap. In 2015, he and Michelle launched *Let Girls Learn* (2015) to expand educational opportunities for girls across the globe. From the beginning to the end of his Presidency, and beyond, he worked to demonstrate how a male leader could help to address gender inequality. In his final year in office, he convened and spoke at the United State of Women summit, declaring 'this is what a feminist looks like' (Obama, 2016). He expanded on the topic in August 2016: 'we need to keep changing the attitude that raises our girls to be demure and our boys to be assertive, that criticises our daughters for speaking out and our sons for shedding a tear'. He modelled this modern masculinity repeatedly, shedding tears in public, foregrounding and amplifying powerful and successful women, including his wife Michelle. Of his daughters he said: 'it's important that their dad is a feminist, because now that's what they expect of all men'. Barack Obama is what a #HeForShe role model looks like.

ORGANISATIONAL STRUCTURES

#HEFORSHE LEADERSHIP AT CHURCHILL ACADEMY & SIXTH FORM

As the headteacher of a large secondary school in North Somerset, I have worked hard to promote gender equality across the Academy. This has included, but is not limited to:

- Ensuring equal representation on the senior leadership team (split 50:50 female:male)
- Rotating the chair at SLT meetings and laying down explicit expectations in terms of contribution and discussion
- Revising the attendance management and leave of absence policies to be more family friendly
- Accommodating flexible working requests wherever possible from male and female colleagues
- Implementing a transgender policy to ensure fair access and treatment for all, and using gender-neutral pronouns in policy documentation and statements ('they' instead of 'he/she') to remove the notion of a gender binary
- Ensuring aspiring women leaders are coached and developed through our Teaching School Alliance's Women into Leadership programme
- Actively promoting #WomenEd and encouraging colleagues to participate in the regional network
- Ensuring colleagues participate in the Women Leading in Education coaching programme and regional network coordinated by the Department for Education

The combination of these approaches has begun the process of moving the school towards gender equality in leadership. Although the systemic, societal and cultural pressures and expectations are high, we have to start somewhere: we have started here.

CHANGING THE SYSTEM

- Can you ensure that women's voices are not just heard but amplified in your school?
- Can you ensure that female role models are afforded equal prominence to males in your curriculum, assemblies and school environment?
- Can you check your own privilege, identify your own implicit biases and work to counteract them?
- If not you, then who? If not now, then when?

REFERENCES

Burgess, S. (2016a) 'How Michelle Obama's visit to a London school helped boost students' grades', *The Conversation*, July [Online]. Available at: http://theconversation.com/how-michelle-obamas-visit-to-a-london-school-helped-boost-students-grades-61694 (accessed 17 February 2018).

Burgess, S. (2016b) *Michelle Obama and an English School: The Power of Inspiration*, Research Evidence in Education [Online]. Available at: http://simonburgesseconomics.co.uk/wp-content/uploads/2016/06/EGA-paper-20160627.pdf (accessed 17 February 2018).

Department for Education (2017) *School Workforce in England – November 2016*. Available at: www.gov.uk/government/statistics/school-workforce-in-england-november-2016 (accessed 12 February 2018).

Goddard, V. (2014) *The Best Job in the World*. Carmarthen: Crown House Publishing.

Landsbaum, C. (2016) 'Obama's female staffers came up with a genius strategy to make sure their voices were heard', *The Cut*, 13 September [Online]. Available at: www.thecut.com/2016/09/heres-how-obamas-female-staffers-made-their-voices-heard.html (accessed 18 February 2018).

Lean In (n.d) LeanIn.org [Online] Available at: https://leanin.org/ (accessed 18 February 2018).

Lean In (2018a) *Get the most out of meetings*, Lean In [Online]. Available at: https://leanin.org/tips/mvp#tip4 (accessed 17 February 2018).

Lean In (2018b) *7 Tips for Men Who Want To Support Equality*, Lean In [Online]. Available at: https://leanin.org/tips/mvp (accessed 17 February 2018).

Lean In (2018c) *#MentorHer Survey Results: Key Findings*, Lean In [Online]. Available at: https://leanin.org/sexual-harassment-backlash-survey-results/ (accessed 17 February 2018).

Leaper, C. and Ayres, M. (2007) 'A meta-analytic review of gender variations in adults' language use: Talkativeness, affiliative speech, and assertive speech', *Personal and Social Psychology Review*, *11*(4): 328–363.

Let Girls Learn (2015) Let Girls Learn [Online]. Available at: https://letgirlslearn.gov/about (accessed 18 February 2018).

Obama, B. (2016) 'This is what a feminist looks like', *Glamour*, August [Online]. Available at: www.glamour.com/story/glamour-exclusive-president-barack-obama-says-this-is-what-a-feminist-looks-like (accessed 18 February 2018).

Obama, M. (2009) 'Speech at Elizabeth Garett Anderson School', *YouTube*, April [Online]. Available at: https://youtu.be/1fEOWFHtozU (accessed 17 February 2018).

Sandberg, S. (2010) 'Why we have too few women leaders', *TED.com*, December [Online]. Available at: www.ted.com/talks/sheryl_sandberg_why_we_have_too_few_women_leaders (accessed 15 February 2018).

Stocking, B. and Armstrong, J. (2016) *Collaborating with Men: From Research to Day-to-Day Practice*, Murray Edwards College [Online]. Available at: www.murrayedwards.cam.ac.uk/sites/default/files/files/Report%202%20-%20Collaborating%20with%20Men%20July%202017.pdf (accessed 18 February 2018).

UN Women (2016) 'Take action: Education', *HeForShe* [Online]. Available at: www.heforshe.org/en/take-action/education (accessed 15 February 2018).

UNESCO (2015) *A Guide for Gender Equality in Teacher Education Policy and Practices*. Available at: http://unesdoc.unesco.org/images/0023/002316/231646e.pdf (accessed 15 February 2018).

Watson, E. (2014a) 'Emma Watson at the HeForShe Campaign, 2014 Official UN Video', *YouTube*, September [Online]. Available at: https://youtu.be/gkjW9PZBRfk (accessed 15 February 2018).

Watson, E. (2014b) 'Gender equality is your issue too', *UN Women*, September [Online]. Available at: www.unwomen.org/en/news/stories/2014/9/emma-watson-gender-equality-is-your-issue-too (accessed 15 February 2018).

Wheaton, W. (2012) 'Happy don't be a dick day!', *wilwheaton.net*, 29 July. Available at: http://wilwheaton.net/2012/07/happy-dont-be-a-dick-day/ (accessed 17 February 2018).

10

FLEXING OUR SCHOOLS

HELENA MARSH AND CAROLINE DERBYSHIRE

KEY POINTS

This chapter will cover:

- Fostering a flexible working culture in our school communities

- Communicating a commitment to recruiting and retaining great people

- Supporting flexible parental leave and leadership opportunities

- Challenging unrealistic workload expectations

- Collaborating to make flexible working work

INTRODUCTION

In 2017, the Department for Education in England updated its policy paper on flexible working in schools for good reason: the teaching profession is rapidly heading towards a staffing crisis. The high proportion of teachers leaving teaching within the first five years not only is creating retention issues for schools, but constitutes a huge waste of the public money used to train teachers in the first place. Retaining staff through flexible working is what Timewise describes as a 'talent imperative' (Timewise, 2017).

The Department for Education (2018) defines flexible working as:

- Part-time working – working less than full-time hours
- Job-sharing
- Compressed hours – working full-time, but over fewer days
- Staggered hours – with different start, finish and break times
- Home working

Ironically, teaching has traditionally been perceived as a family-friendly career or one that enables the pursuit of wider interests. Long holidays and the short school day have been seen as pleasantly compatible with being a parent or carer or pursuing hobbies, but there are many dimensions to teaching that undermine this notional flexibility.

The rigidity of the set timetable and the envelope of the school day can deny the teacher any time off during term time, making managing day-to-day human needs challenging. It is not possible to postpone fixing that gushing bath tap until the next holiday, for example, or do anything about the family holiday inconveniently scheduled on a Friday.

With a set timetable, any notion of 'flexi-time' is often seen as impossible. Furthermore, teachers have to arrive in school early and often have meetings after school, followed by a considerable takeaway workload of planning, marking and administration. Holidays may be generous, but much of this free time is used to catch up with assessment or get ahead with planning the next term. Anyone who shares their house with a teacher will tell you how significant the teacher workload is and how very dully it dominates conversation and home life!

It is for these very reasons that many teachers are keen to explore the idea of flexible contracts. Headteachers need to balance the needs of the school with those of individual colleagues. Part-time working could have the perceived undesirable impact of split classes, complicated timetabling, increasing recruitment costs and disruption to learning. It is also true to say that there are some serious disincentives for those seeking part-time teaching. The UK Institute for Fiscal Studies, in February 2018, reported that mothers in part-time jobs are often not given pay rises linked to experience, and that by the time a couple's first child is 20, many mothers earn a third less than the fathers. This contributes significantly to the gender pay gap.

However, the consequences for schools in not engaging with flexible working massively outweigh these considerations. In the English education context, where one in three teachers does not remain in the profession beyond the first three years, retaining teachers is a top priority. A flexible working arrangement might make the difference between a teacher feeling that the work–life juggle is manageable and feeling so overwhelmed that they give up on the profession entirely.

FOSTERING A FLEXIBLE WORKING CULTURE IN OUR SCHOOL COMMUNITIES

#WomenEd recognises that education is behind the curve in seriously engaging with flexible working. In order for the benefits of flexible working to be fully embraced by schools, the attitudes of leaders and governors need to change. The co-founder of Timewise, Karen Mattison (2018), has commented that 'all it takes is an open-minded employer who is prepared to try something new in a bid to hire or keep the best people', but in the context of schools too few are convinced of the benefits of flexible working. School culture dances to the rhythm of the supply and demand beats of a rigid timetable, but surely this must now change.

According to the 2017 ComRes survey of 3001 adults, 92% of young workers want flexible approaches to working. They want it far more than their older counterparts, and both men and women are motivated by the prospect of flexible employment. This is not because the younger generation are not prepared to work hard, but because they quite rightly want a more balanced approach to life and work. One in ten people in England are now what the Office for National Statistics classifies as overemployed: they are working more than they wish to or than is healthy for them or the nation.

If flexible working is to become the norm in teaching, we need to change the working culture in schools. In some, the idea of a part-time member of the middle or senior leadership team is not even entertained. In many, teachers are not respected if they leave school early to attend to caring or childcare responsibilities and are expected to stay at school late and be visible to their colleagues. Headteachers must set a positive example; they should actively discourage presenteeism and remove the taboos associated with working from home by modelling its effectiveness. Staff members should be encouraged to use technology to support flexible approaches to working.

This change in culture must be communicated and celebrated openly in the school community. As Jill Berry (2018) in her Teachtalks article points out, flexible working will only become a reality if school leaders adopt a 'How can we try to make this work?' approach rather than hiding behind the challenges.

COMMUNICATING A COMMITMENT TO RECRUITING AND RETAINING GREAT PEOPLE

In October 2017, more than 60 organisations, including #WomenEd, pledged to encourage schools to introduce more flexible working practices. The *Tes* committed to ensure that all job advertisements on its website clearly display whether the school will accept job-share or flexible working solutions. Timewise's research reveals that only one in ten of all current job advertisements (teaching and support staff) in the UK make it explicit that flexible working is a possibility (Mattison, 2018).

#WomenEd is working with the Chartered College of Teaching, the Association of School and College Leaders (ASCL) and other organisations to develop case studies of successful working practices to share with the sector. This move acknowledges that headteachers' values are key to any change. One of the easiest improvements that our schools have made is to include a sentence about flexible working opportunities in all job advertisements, including those for senior posts. Furthermore, all applicants are reassured that conversations about flexibility will not prejudice the selection outcome.

Charles Dickens Primary in London recognises that the attitude of parents towards shared classes also needs to be addressed to help them to understand the very many benefits of retaining talented colleagues. The school's headteacher, quoted in the *Tes* (2017), communicates the positives with great clarity:

> For us, flexible working is allowing our staff team to lead full lives and work for us. I want to be able to retain good, ambitious teachers, to support staff pursuing postgraduate degrees or other interests and to acknowledge that the impact of each employee is not based on how many hours they are in the building but on how effective they are and how well our children are doing.

A lack of flexibility negatively impacts on women in particular: 91% of women in the workforce would prefer to work flexibly, according to the ComRes survey in 2017. This is 7% higher than the male response to the same question. An analysis of the school workforce by the Policy Exchange thinktank (2016) found that around one in four teachers who quit the classroom in recent years were women aged between 30 and 39. Given that 73% of the teaching workforce are female, this figure is particularly concerning. The perception that a teaching career is not compatible with family life must be addressed by employers. Jonathan Simmons, author of the paper published by ASCL (2016), expressed particular concern, saying 'Our education system needs to embrace a new way of working' (BBC, 2016).

SUPPORTING FLEXIBLE PARENTAL LEAVE AND LEADERSHIP OPPORTUNITIES

Shared parental leave has been identified as crucial to addressing the gender pay gap and supporting women's career progression. Legislation introduced in the UK in April 2015 enabling parents to share statutory leave has had minimal uptake so far, with only around 3% of eligible couples taking advantage of the scheme in its first year (BBC, 2018). This is a stark contrast to Scandinavian 'latte dads' culture where parental leave is offered up to eight years after a child's birth (Kane, 2018).

It is also necessary to challenge existing, binary approaches to maternity and paternity leave, as exemplified by the inspiring work of the Maternity Teacher Paternity Teacher Project (see: www.mtpt.org.uk). Emma Sheppard launched #MTPT via Twitter in June 2016 when her first child was born to engage with professional learning during her break from teaching. Emma is a strong advocate of flexible parental leave and the importance of supporting teachers to make personal choices about their time off, keeping in touch with practices and return to work:

> There is no right way to 'do' parental leave or a one size fits all model. Some teachers want to cut off completely from work when on leave, whereas others might enjoy using their leave as an opportunity for professional development. For both the schools and teachers the key to ensuring that individuals feel fulfilled during this time is open and transparent dialogue that invites them to communicate their needs.

Emma also articulates how influential a school's treatment of those on leave can be on teacher retention:

> Taking care of women while they are on parental leave is the first step in ensuring that they do not fall victim to the motherhood penalty, stagnate in their careers, or drop out of teaching altogether. And it's important to remember that 'taking care of teachers' means different things for different people. It could be inviting a teacher to interview for a promoted position, ensuring that they are paid a fair rate for their Keeping in Touch (KIT) days or leaving them well alone and welcoming them back with open arms when they decide to return. (Brighouse et al., 2018)

Emma's words above are reported in the Brighouse et al. article in the *Tes*'s 'What to expect when you are expecting' (2018) issue, which contains case studies and advice including how to make the most of KIT days, employees' legal rights and tips for navigating and negotiating the return to work.

Essentially, headteachers must not be constrained by received wisdom about working patterns but instead think about more pressing priorities: retaining excellent staff. Surprisingly, the only retention tactic used by many schools is to offer financial incentives rather than considering flexible working. Many heads shoehorn employees into a rigid system in the interests of parity of experience rather than mould systems around the needs of their employees. Schools are often slow to challenge orthodoxies about employment, yet employee loyalty can be built by allowing employees to manage their workload flexibly or by making small adjustments, showing care for and trust in their staff.

CASE STUDY: CAROLINE DERBYSHIRE

Caroline Derbyshire is CEO of Saffron Academy Trust in Essex.

> My own experience of leadership in education reinforces the argument for flexible approaches. I returned to work four months after my second child was born and took on my first senior leadership position in 2000. The post was tailor-made for me and although I knew it would be very difficult to manage while I had a small baby and also a toddler, I knew that few men would ever accept that being a new parent meant that they could not be ambitious.
>
> I demanded equality, but it was not easy. In fact, I contemplated giving up my job entirely at regular intervals, but I was blessed with a headteacher whose own daughter was experiencing the same

challenges as a working mother and he enabled me to work short days for a set period and, when my eldest started school, permitted me to leave at lunchtime once a fortnight so that I could keep in touch with the reception class teacher. These tiny flexibilities meant the world to me and allowed me to cope when without them I might not have done so. As a result, he retained a senior leader who has gone on to become a headteacher and then a system leader. Another headteacher might have been obsessed with how these gestures were perceived by others, or whether he was setting up a difficult precedent. I was fortunate to work for someone whose eyes were on the bigger prize.

As a headteacher, I recognise that slight timetable adjustments for new parents can bring huge benefits. A later start with a protected free period, an afternoon of working at home, the permission to attend a child's school events: none of these things are difficult to give but denial of them is what drives many women to abandon the workplace or feel that a part-time role is their only viable option.

Affordable and convenient childcare which accommodates the early starts of the school day is also a frequent barrier to remaining in employment or career progression as a teaching mother. As a deputy headteacher, I helped to establish a workplace nursery on the school site that accepted babies as young as 4 months and opened from 7.30am to 6.30pm. It offered preferential rates and priority bookings to school staff. My own son was one of its first clients and the nursery has remained invaluable for working teachers at the school ever since. Two of my current female senior leadership team colleagues also used places for their growing families.

As CEO, I remain determined to take an engaged and positive approach to flexible working for all. Our Trust's flexible working policy states a commitment to giving serious consideration to all requests as an integral part of recruiting and retaining the very best teachers.

CHALLENGING UNREALISTIC WORKLOAD EXPECTATIONS

Accommodating flexible working requests may help to quell the tide of teachers leaving the profession, but it does not necessarily address endemic issues. As research from England's Department for Education (2018) has revealed, the root cause of many teachers wishing to opt for a reduction in their contact time is to attempt to make teaching do-able. Therefore, while schools need to be receptive to flexible working opportunities, they also need to be careful that, as Michael Tidd asserts, 'paying teachers to teach part-time and work on their days off isn't the only way of keeping the job manageable' (2018).

In times of budgetary austerity it may be appealing to pay teachers part time for full-time commitment, but this is neither ethical nor sustainable. Teaching is a vocation, but that does not grant it permission to be all-consuming. Teaching should be compatible with life for those with or without caring responsibilities, not solely for those who are able and willing to subscribe to exhausting conditions and/or choose to sacrifice a full-time salary or their personal lives.

In 2014 over 44,000 teachers responded to the Department for Education's Workload Challenge survey, highlighting the volume and pressure of tasks that they have to contend with: data tracking, intervention classes, mock inspections, emails, in addition to routine planning, preparation and marking. Understandably, many teachers in England craved additional non-contact time in which to keep on top of duties.

#WomenEd recognises that workload demands have affected recruitment and retention in leadership roles as well as teaching positions. Teachers struggling to cope with the day-to-day demands of the classroom may not have the appetite to step up to roles involving additional responsibility.

We need to directly challenge the prevailing work culture in many schools that considers full-time teachers who work late and visibly at school to be the most conscientious professionals. We also need to tackle teacher workload by removing unnecessary tasks and addressing unhealthy accountability pressures in order to stem the dire retention consequences for the profession.

COLLABORATING TO MAKE FLEXIBLE WORKING WORK

It is important that both employer and employee are reasonable and realistic when balancing flexible working needs and wishes. While it may not be feasible to promise teachers the degree of flexibility afforded in other industries, a resistance to flexible working on the grounds of business reasons underestimates potential benefits to schools' finances and standards.

Nevertheless, even the most skilful school timetablers will struggle to manage a significant proportion of 'inflexible' flexible working requests, for example the need for 60% teaching allocation to be Tuesday–Thursday or only teaching between the hours of 9am and 2pm. Although prospective part-timers will, understandably, want to condense their working time and co-ordinate it with other commitments, fulfilling individuals' exacting requirements may be to the detriment of being able to accommodate a number of flexible working requests.

Pushing for change in childcare, in addition to other employment sectors, is an important part of achieving effective flexible working for teachers. Many new parents are constricted not only by the structural demands of their own schools, but by inflexible and limited childcare options and partners' rigid working arrangements. Affordable wraparound childcare and flexible nursery and pre-school provision is essential for teaching parents, as is the ability for both parents to benefit from flexible working arrangements.

CASE STUDY: HELENA MARSH

Helena Marsh is Executive Principal of Chilford Hundred Education Trust and Linton Village College in Cambridgeshire.

I had my first child in the second term of my first assistant headship. I was keen to return to work full time and my (non-teaching) partner, now husband, and I decided it would be best if he could reduce his hours to be the primary carer for at least two days a week.

His flexible working request was initially rejected, despite the fact that returning mothers in his department had been granted similar requests. He appealed the decision and was eventually successful in securing a job share.

Finding a suitable nursery was another challenge. We initially explored childcare institutions close to home but travel implications and opening hours proved problematic, as did nurseries' inflexibility in school holidays.

Eventually we identified a setting close to my school that was open from 7.30am-6pm, enabling me to drop off and pick up my daughter. When our son was born, my husband cared for him when I returned to my new senior leadership role when he was three and a half months old.

My husband's flexible working arrangements enabled me to manage my career with a young family. Having a 'real partner' (as Sheryl Sandberg puts it), workable childcare and the understanding of great headteachers was crucial to my professional development.

Personal experience of the challenges of juggling teaching, leadership and life have given me a greater sense of empathy and understanding with my own staff and their flexible working wishes. As headteacher, I have granted many requests for part-time working/job shares, supported shared parental leave and have approved tweaks to working patterns to accommodate teachers' family commitments and personal circumstances.

It can be easy to view flexible working arrangements as inconvenient. Having over a third of our teachers, including many middle leaders, working part time certainly creates significant timetabling challenges for the deputy principal but our staff are human beings with personal lives and needs; we neglect this at our peril.

FLEXIBLE WORKING IN ORGANISATIONS

The change in legislation in 2014 to allow all employees the right to request flexible working after 26 weeks, without specific caring responsibilities, marked an important shift in its accessibility. However, it has taken time for the education sector to respond to this.

Intelligent and creative timetabling is needed to address historic working practices in schools. It is too easy to fall back to a 'computer says no' excuse. In the short-term, there may be additional costs and considerations to accommodate flexible working practices, but it is necessary to invest in such practices to safeguard the future of the profession.

Only 27% of those who have recently left teaching are retiring and half of all teachers who have left teaching to raise families have not returned. There is also the long-term organisational benefit of not having to recruit and train teachers to replace those leaving; an estimated £1.3 billion a year is being paid to supply agencies to staff England's schools, and 600,000 students are currently taught lessons by unqualified teachers (Pells, 2017).

Holly Power, founder of Return to Teach, a UK organisation that campaigns for and coordinates flexible working for teachers, was driven to action having witnessed the impact of the retention crisis on her own students' education and on a national scale. Return to Teach is working to redress the issue that there are currently more qualified teachers out of classrooms in England than in them. Its website platform matches experienced teachers with schools offering flexible working (see https://returntoteach.co.uk).

Schools need to tackle the challenges posed by flexible working in order to achieve a timetable that is manageable and maintains high standards of teaching and learning. Fair, open and transparent decision-making and communication are central to this process. Having clear flexible working policies in place is an important first step.

Flexible working has become synonymous with working part time. While this kind of working pattern may be entirely appropriate for a proportion of the teaching population, it is not feasible or desirable for all teachers' circumstances. If the day job is perceived as being unmanageable, however many days are worked, the demanding nature of teaching may be deemed incompatible with teachers' extra-curricular commitments and lifestyles.

Furthermore, an increase in the number of part-time teachers could create further wholesale systematic issues. Laura McInerney (2018) speculates a need for an additional 40,000 teachers if 40% of the current teaching population were to reduce to working four days a week. While we cannot rely on part-time working to get us out of the current teacher recruitment and retention crisis, neither can we ignore the institutional factors that have led to it becoming so appealing to teachers.

School leadership has a significant role to play in ensuring that teachers' workload is realistic and achievable and that staff are trusted to manage their workload in a flexible way. Colleagues at every level in an organisation need to tackle the martyrdom that can creep into staffrooms (or, more likely, isolated classrooms and homes).

Open communication is needed about how teaching can be achieved flexibly, not only through part-time and job-share arrangements, but also through an appreciation of different ways of working such as using non-contact time flexibly, accommodating later starts or earlier finishes, and encouraging teachers to not judge themselves or each other by how many hours they spend in the school building.

ROLE MODELS: SUE BROWN AND RACHAEL SCHOFIELD

Sue Brown and Rachael Schofield are headteachers of Bassingbourn Community Primary School in Cambridgeshire and National Leaders of Education.

Two heads are better than one, literally! Sue and Rachael demonstrate how it is possible to make flexible working manageable and use it to enable system leadership.

Since starting as co-heads at their primary school in 2011, Sue and Rachael have extended their influence to other schools. Leading a National Support School, they have both facilitated Teaching School professional learning and have led school to school improvement projects in addition to their day jobs as headteachers and mums. Working two and a half days each has helped both of them to make the leadership role compatible with their family lives and has also given them capacity to engage in wider leadership consultancy and freelance projects.

Sue and Rachael have a fantastic working relationship; they share core values and principles and also bring different, complementary skills and expertise to the headship. Their school benefits from having two energetic and committed leaders and the wider perspective from their work in other establishments.

Setting the flexible working tone from the top helps to tackle the assumption that students will suffer from job-share arrangements. Communication is key to ensure the smooth running of a school; Sue and Rachael's leadership demonstrates that flexible working challenges are surmountable and can actually present opportunities. They are honest about the fact that they would not be school leaders if the co-headship had not been possible. While this poses a question about whether expectations of headship are reasonable, it also highlights the potential lost leaders who exist as a result of inflexible approaches to teaching and leadership.

CHANGING THE SYSTEM

- What flexible working practices can you develop to recruit and retain excellent staff?
- What can school leaders do to foster a culture in which a healthy and realistic workload is actively encouraged?
- How can flexible leadership work successfully in schools for the benefit of staff and students?
- How can we tackle the inherent rigidity of school structures to accommodate and support flexible working arrangements, such as co-ordinating prospective job share applicants?
- How can we address historic issues, prejudices and barriers in education and other sectors to safeguard the future of our profession?

REFERENCES

ASCL (2016) *New Research: Working Women are Quitting Teaching for Good*, ASCL, 4 March [Online]. Available at: www.ascl.org.uk/news-and-views/news_news-detail.new-research-working-women-are-quitting-teaching-for-good.html (accessed 23 June 2018).

BBC (2016) 'Flexible working could help solve teacher shortage, think tank argues', *BBC News*, 4 March [Online]. Available at: www.bbc.co.uk/news/education-35718553 (accessed 23 June 2018).

BBC (2018) 'Shared parental leave take-up may be as low as 2%', *BBC News*, 12 February [Online]. Available at: www.bbc.co.uk/news/business-43026312 (accessed 23 June 2018).

Berry, J. (2018) 'Flexible working . . . dream or reality?' *Teachtalks* [Online]. Available at: http://teachtalks.co.uk/flexible-working-dream-or-reality/ (accessed 23 June 2018).

Brighouse, J., Merrit, L., Sheppard, E. and Starbuck Braidley, L. (2018) 'Becoming a parent: Returning to work', *Tes* 30 March [Online]. Available at: www.tes.com/news/tes-magazine/tes-magazine/becoming-a-parent-returning-work (accessed 23 June 2018).

ComRes (2017) *Timewise Flexible Working Survey*, ComRes, 19 September [Online]. Available at: www.comresglobal.com/wp-content/uploads/2017/09/Timewise-Flexible-Working-Survey-Data-Tables.pdf (accessed 23 June 2018).

Department for Education (2018) *Exploring Teacher Workload: Qualitative Research* [Online]. Available at: https://assets.publishing.service.gov.uk/government/uploads/system/uploads/attachment_data/file/593990/DFE_Flex_Working_Guidance_2017_FINAL.pdf (accessed 23 June 2018).

Institute for Fiscal Studies (2018) *Mothers Suffer Long-term Pay Penalty from Part-time Working*, IFS, 5 February [Online]. Available at: www.ifs.org.uk/publications/10364 (accessed 23 June 2018).

Kane, L. (2018) 'Sweden is apparently full of "latte dads" carrying toddlers – and it's a sign of critical social change', *Business Insider UK*, 4 April [Online]. Available at: http://uk.businessinsider.com/sweden-maternity-leave-paternity-leave-policies-latte-dads-2018-4 (accessed 23 June 2018).

Mattison, K. (2018) *Timewise Joint CEO Karen Mattison MBE on Flexible Working, the Timewise Power 50 and the New Work-Less Movement*, Women's Business Council, 26 February [Online]. Available at: www.womensbusinesscouncil.co.uk/karen-mattison-article/ (accessed 23 June 2018).

McInerney, L. (2018) 'Flexible working sounds lovely, but it would make the teacher shortage worse', *The Guardian*, 20 February [Online]. Available at: www.theguardian.com/education/2018/feb/20/flexible-working-teacher-shortage-laura-mcinerney (accessed 23 June 2018).

Pells, R. (2017) 'More than 600,000 pupils being taught lessons by unqualified teachers, says Labour', *Independent*, 25 July [Online]. Available at www.independent.co.uk/news/education/education-news/more-than-600000-half-million-pupils-being-taught-lessons-by-unqualified-teachers-labour-party-maths-a7859831.html (accessed 23 June 2018).

Policy Exchange (2016) *The Importance of Teachers* (ed. J. Simons). Available at: https://policyexchange.org.uk/wp-content/uploads/2016/09/the-Importance-of-Teachers.pdf (accessed 17 October 2018).

Sandberg, S. (2013) *Lean In: Women, Work, and the Will to Lead*. New York: Alfred A. Knopf.

Tes (2017) 'More than 60 organisations pledge action to boost flexible working for teachers', 11 December. Available at: www.tes.com/news/more-60-organisations-pledge-action-boost-flexible-working-teachers (accessed 16 July 2018).

Tidd, M. (2018) 'Teachers go part time just to cut their work load', *Tes* 6 March [Online]. Available at: www.tes.com/news/school-news/breaking-views/teachers-go-part-time-just-cut-their-workload (accessed 23 June 2018).

Timewise (2017) *The Rise of Generation Job Share*, 30 January. Available at: https://timewise.co.uk/article/press-release-the-rise-of-generation-job-share/ (accessed 16 July 2018).

11

WHAT PRICE EQUALITY?:
THE GENDER PAY GAP

VIVIENNE PORRITT

KEY POINTS

This chapter will cover:

- What is the gender pay gap in education?

- Why do we have a gender pay gap?

- How to reduce and eradicate the gender pay gap

INTRODUCTION

One of the issues on which #WomenEd has offered clarity is the gender pay gap. Education, especially in schools and academies, is a feminised workforce yet proportionately fewer women hold senior leadership positions: this has been the case for a long time. This underrepresentation is replicated in universities for both vice chancellors and professors. In 2015, Education Datalab published *Seven Things You Might Not Know About Our Schools*, which analysed UK teachers working full time across two years of the workforce (2010 and 2011) and demonstrated that women who gain senior leadership roles are paid less than men with a similar responsibility (see Figure 11.1).

Figure 11.1 Gender pay gap, 2015 (Education Datalab, 2015)

This new clarity about the gender pay gap was one of the key challenges that #WomenEd faced head on. When I share the data in Figure 11.1 at #WomenEd events, most participants stare at it with a puzzled look on their face, then become shocked, angry or more uncertain. The usual question is 'How can this be?'. In the United Kingdom, data on the gender pay gap required by the government elicits the same question as do the international league tables on the gender pay gap.

This chapter aims to answer the question 'How can there be a pay gap in education?' and suggests ways we can reduce and ultimately eradicate the gap.

WHAT IS THE GENDER PAY GAP?

First, the gender pay gap does not refer to equal pay. In the United Kingdom, men and women performing equal work in the same employment must receive equal pay as legislated in the

Equal Pay Act of 1970 and the Equality Act 2010. Equal pay includes all aspects of benefits, including bonuses or performance-related salary increases. Equal pay is a principle in the European Union, the US, Australia and Canada.

The gender pay gap shows the difference in the average pay between all men and women in an organisation. In the UK, the gender pay gap shows the difference between the *average* (mean) gross hourly earnings and the *middle* (median) ranking person in terms of pay for women and men. Positive percentages mean men earn more than women in the organisation or the sector's workforce. The UK government requires all organisations with 250+ employees in England, Scotland or Wales to publish their gender pay gap data on their website and report this data to the government.

To see how this works in the UK, Table 11.1 shows an anonymous example from the 2018 gender pay gap report from a group of schools that form a large multi-academy trust (MAT) in England.

Table 11.1 Anonymous MAT gender pay gap data, 2018, percentages rounded

Mean (average) gap	Median (middle) gap	Bonus pay received – women	Bonus pay received –men	Mean bonus gap	Median bonus gap
18%	19%	60%	68%	39%	31%

Source: based on anonymised data from https://gender-pay-gap.service.gov.uk/

The gender pay gap, as shown in Table 11.1, means the mean hourly rate for women is 18% lower than that for men. Women's median hourly rate is 19% lower than men's. Women were in the majority in each of the four quartiles, ranging from 60% in the highest paid quartile to 81% in the lowest paid quartile. Whilst the number of women (60%) who received a bonus compared to men (68%) is more equal, women's mean bonus pay is 39% lower than men so men received significantly larger bonuses than women.

Sadly, this is a similar picture across most of the education organisations that reported their gender pay data. This led to the education sector being ranked third in the UK league table of sectors with the largest gender pay gaps, alongside the construction and finance and insurance sectors which, traditionally, have a masculinised workforce. I feel this is shameful. The BBC (2018a) and many others reported that '40 of the 100 companies with the biggest pay gap are primary or secondary schools with 10 of those having a median pay gap of 50% or higher'.

I believe that educational organisations pride themselves on being inclusive, fair employers who want to improve lives and who believe in equality and equity. I'd find a combination of these words in the mission statement of most schools, academies, further education colleges or universities. Yet 'women working in academy chains suffer some of the worst gender pay gaps in the UK' according to *The Guardian*'s analysis (Adams and Duncan, 2018). The *Tes* reported that the difference between what men and women earn in schools and academies in 2018 is higher than the UK average: 18.8% compared to the national figure of 13.1% as reported on 20 March 2018 (Ward, 2018). The BBC (2018b) reported that across all universities in England, the average gender pay gap is 18.4%. In education's feminised workforce, shouldn't we be more equitable than other sectors?

It is important to say there are issues with this approach to describing the gender pay data. It is complex: the UK government requires the information to be broken down into 14 separate data points; firms such as lawyers and management consultants don't count equity partners, who tend to be very well-paid men; and large corporate groups have several subsidiaries who report separately. All of this means the gender pay gap may be less or more, depending on how the data is structured.

Nevertheless, this is a great deal more data about salaries than we have had previously. The evidence for the gender pay gap suggests to me that women who aspire to or who hold a leadership role are not treated equitably in our education workforce, despite the mission statements displayed by their employers. *The Guardian* said the UK data-gathering exercise reveals 'structural inequality of opportunity' (Topping et al., 2018). What price equality for women in education?

WHY DO WE HAVE A GENDER PAY GAP?

I hope that the starkness of the UK's gender pay gap in education will spark significant change. We need education employers to look at the barriers facing women's progression in the workplace. According to Sam Smethers, Chief Executive of the Fawcett Society, as reported in *The Guardian* (Topping et al., 2018), awareness of the size of the pay gap is 'a game changer. It forces employers to look at themselves and understand their organisations and it prompts employees to ask some hard questions'.

The first question to ask is, why are we in this position? The reasons are, as Fuller (2017) states, 'a complex range of interacting factors'. I am exploring three, in particular:

- underrepresentation
- unconscious bias
- confidence

UNDERREPRESENTATION

The proportional underrepresentation of women at leadership levels in schools has been demonstrated in Chapter 1, and the lack of Black, Asian and Ethnic Minority women is highlighted in Chapter 5. This lack of representation of women in leadership contributes to the 12% gender pay gap for academic university staff as cited by the University and College Union: 'The large gender imbalance among senior academic staff is a primary driver of the intransigent gender pay gap' (UCU, 2017: iv).

Research into how quickly men and women teachers reach their first leadership role shows it is similar in secondary schools and more pronounced in primary schools with men achieving this after six years or less, compared to nine years or less for women (Department for Education, 2018). And, from data produced by Rebecca Allen (2018), Director of the Centre for Education Improvement Science, UCL Institute of Education, men reach senior leader roles and headship faster than women in both primary and secondary schools, as seen in Figure 11.2.

Fuller argues strongly that 'women's underrepresentation in headship is a matter of social injustice' (2017: 55). In her survey of the local authorities in England, only 'seven authorities had a proportion of women secondary headteachers that matches the proportion of women secondary teachers nationally' (2017: 57).

Women are also underrepresented as chief executive officers (CEOs) in academy trusts, the new level of senior leadership in English schools. Fuller (2017: 56) highlights that 'the majority of chief executive officers of the large chains of academies are men'. Male CEOs also lead larger trusts, and trustees – who appoint and reward CEOs – are also mostly men

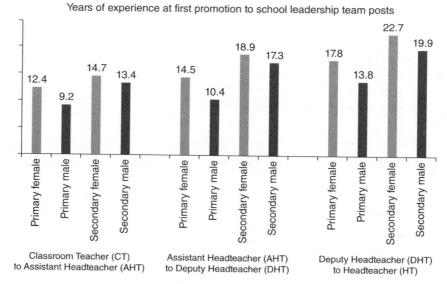

Figure 11.2 Men reach headship faster than women (Allen, 2018)

(Mansell, 2016; Staufenberg, 2018). The outcome, in April 2018, was that 'across the 16 trusts headed by men with 20 or more schools, the average CEO salary was £174,765. Across those headed by women, the average salary was £139,800 – almost £35,000 less' (Staufenberg, 2018). And according to Education Datalab (Nye, 2018), across 471 academy trusts 'the average gender pay gap was 31.7 per cent in men's favour. That is, for every £100 earned by a man, £68.30p was earned by a woman'.

These issues immediately influence the gender pay gap, as men earn higher wages for reaching leadership posts earlier and there are more male leaders in secondary schools and academy trusts where salaries are higher. Basically, in a feminised workforce, men are present in greater numbers the higher up the organisation you go. It seems equity in education will come at a very large cost.

UNCONSCIOUS BIAS

A simple, yet rigorous, experiment explains unconscious bias. In 2012, researchers from Yale University asked male and female staff from the science faculties of six anonymous universities to rate identical CVs to hire a laboratory manager. The researchers randomly assigned either a male, John, or a female name, Jennifer, to the CVs. Not only was John hired by more people, he was also offered a higher starting salary than Jennifer. Women and men were equally likely to exhibit bias against the female student. In this experiment, the researchers found that 'subtle bias against women was associated with less support for the female student but was unrelated to reactions to the male student' (Moss-Racusin et al., 2012: 1).

As this study shows, both women and men have unconscious biases. We are influenced by a mass of information from our experiences and what we read, hear or see. Everyone internalises their own unconscious biases. Girls may be socialised 'not to promote their own interests and to focus instead on the needs of others', as suggested by Babcock et al. (2003).

Unconscious bias is natural and unintended. However, the gender stereotypes, which start from when we are very young, as described in Chapter 3, have a significant influence on our own unconscious bias. In relation to the gender pay gap, this can affect your decisions about applying for a job, and those of employers when they decide to offer you a job and what to pay you.

I'm going to highlight four points in your education career that affect how much you are paid and consider the effects of unconscious bias at each stage.

FIRST JOB

At numerous #WomenEd events, most women said they expected to receive the bottom level of the salary structure related to their very first job. They weren't aware they could discuss or negotiate their starting salary. This chimes with a large body of research suggesting women do not negotiate as much as men. In the study by Babcock et al. (2003), the 'starting salaries of male MBAs who had recently graduated from Carnegie Mellon were 7.6%, or almost $4,000, higher on average than those of female MBAs from the same program'. The authors explain that most of the women had 'simply accepted the employer's initial salary offer; in fact, only 7% had attempted to negotiate. But 57% of their male counterparts – or eight times as many men as women – had asked for more'.

Interestingly, Bowles et al. (2007) found no significant gender differences in negotiation outcomes in industries in which applicants 'had relatively good information about appropriate salary standards'. This suggests we need to tell women that they can discuss their starting salary, especially those moving into education from other sectors or with previous, relevant experience. Education unions have a role to play and #WomenEd is keen to support!

It is important to think about salary from the start of your career. Most employers in education still ask for your current salary when you apply for a new role. The cumulative effects of pay inequality can follow you throughout your career and so affect your pension.

NEW JOB

A new job could be a team leadership role, a senior leader role or headship. You know the salary range offered so what do you do? When I was offered the post of a secondary head-teacher, I beamed and said, 'thank you very much'. I knew there was a salary scale and yet it didn't occur to me to negotiate to start higher up the pay scale; I simply assumed I would start at the lowest rate as I was new to the role. Looking back, I had a convincing case. I'd been a deputy head in a large, split-site school and frequently the sole person out of three in the headship team on either of the sites due to secondment arrangements. When I moved to my next role, I did negotiate successfully, and it was easier than I expected. Think about your own worth when putting your application together, and, when you are successful and offered the job, you can ask for clarification or a discussion about the starting salary. You already know they have spent time deciding you are the best person for the job, so what's the worst that can happen? According to Babcock and Laschever (n.d.), 'When asked to pick metaphors for the process of negotiating, men picked 'winning a ballgame' and a 'wrestling match', while women picked 'going to the dentist'. These gender stereotypes can affect whether you gain the salary you are worth.

PERFORMANCE-RELATED PAY

The third point to influence your salary is whether your pay is related to your performance. Women are still at a disadvantage. Previously, I showed the comparative bonuses in one academy trust in the United Kingdom (Table 11.1 above). Bonuses or salary increases because of performance review are discretionary. Heilman argues that 'because of gender bias and the way in which it influences evaluation in work settings . . . being competent does not ensure that a woman will advance to the same organisational level as an equivalently per-forming man' (2001: 657). Pounders and Coleman's extensive literature review (2002) explores the issues associated with gender and leadership. They ask whether women or men are better leaders and conclude that 'it all depends' (2002: 129). Cecchi-Dimeglio (2017) argues that women are 'shortchanged' by performance reviews. She identified that women were '1.4 times more likely to receive critical subjective feedback (as opposed to either pos-itive feedback or critical objective feedback)'. Such variation in performance reviews could be because 'annual evaluations are often subjective, which opens the door to gender bias' – as Pounder and Coleman suggested, 'it all depends'. Cecchi-Dimeglio's article links back to previous research by Heilman (citing Taylor et al., 1978): 'it has been demonstrated that when actors are of different sexes, the implications drawn from their behaviour is quite different' (2001: 662). Heilman offers examples of such implications, such as 'waiting to make a decision rather than acting immediately may seem passive coming from a woman but prudent coming from a man' (2001: 662).

You can look up the bonuses given to United Kingdom educational organisations at https://gender-pay-gap.service.gov.uk/, and look at the mean and median bonus payments. These and the extensive body of research into gender bias in performance reviews make me question whether the outcomes of annual appraisals are affected by gender stereotypes and unconscious bias.

CAREER BREAK

The fourth career point that can affect your salary is if you have a career break. Chapter 10 looks at flexible working practices in more detail. In terms of the gender pay gap, a career break is likely to reduce your salary, whether it be to care for older parents, to travel or to have children. The latter is the usual reason, with women most likely to take parental leave. Researchers suggest that mothers who are employed account for most of the gender pay gap in wages (Glass, 2004; Corell et al., 2007).

The UK House of Commons Women and Equalities Committee's report on the gender pay gap is also clear that 'women pay a high price for time taken out of work, and this disadvantage persists well beyond the years they spend caring' (2016: 5). This report also notes that 'For female employees, the pay gap between part-time and full-time workers currently stands at 32%' (2016: 13). To be clear, that pay gap is on top of the pay gap for simply being a woman. This is often described as the motherhood penalty.

Simons (2016) highlights the waste of talent due to inflexible options for women school teachers and leaders who have families: 'there is a huge bulge in leavers for women aged between 30–39. In fact, around 6,000 teachers a year – 27% of all leavers in total – are women aged 30–39 (who make up around 23% of the profession overall)' (2016: 17). An Institute for Fiscal Studies (2018) report emphasises that 'the effect of part-time work in shutting down wage progression is especially striking', meaning that part-time working can result in a 'loss of subsequent pay rises'.

The impact of career breaks on women is significant in terms of their personal gender pay gap and across education: 'discrimination, particularly around pregnancy and maternity leave, remains common', according to the website of the Fawcett Society (n.d.). The Fawcett Society believes it will take '100 years to close the gender pay gap'. It may be a longer period for the education sector as it lags behind other sectors in offering flexible working practices that contribute significantly to the gender pay gap.

CONFIDENCE

Is confidence, one of our #WomenEd values, another reason why women are less likely to apply for senior posts and negotiate their salaries or flexible working? The #WomenEd community often reveal personal confidence issues, and Kay and Shipman in 'The confidence gap' (2014) argue that 'there *is* a particular crisis for women – a vast confidence gap that separates the sexes' (emphasis in original). They give examples: 'women don't consider themselves as ready for promotions, they predict they'll do worse on tests, and they generally underestimate their abilities'. So many of our community recognise themselves in these words and realise that they are not the only woman with these fears or the only woman to put limits on what they can achieve. Kay and Shipman go further:

> A review of personnel records found that women working at [Hewlett Packard] applied for a promotion only when they believed they met 100 percent of the qualifications listed for the job. Men were happy to apply when they thought they could meet 60 percent of the job requirements.

'The confidence gap' explores whether confidence matters as much as competence and reluctantly concludes that it does. In the article, male executives 'believed that a lack of confidence was fundamentally holding back women at their companies, but they had shied away from saying anything, because they were terrified of sounding sexist'. No wonder appraisals are crucial in terms of the gender pay gap.

Confidence's big sister is the 'imposter syndrome'. Whilst men do suffer from it, women seem to let their feelings about being an imposter hold them back more than men or are more public about their feelings. Look at Harvard graduate Natalie Portman giving her Harvard Commencement speech in 2015. She shares that she is 'insecure about my own worthiness' as she is just a 'dumb actress'. Whilst writing this chapter, I'm also wondering why any of you would read what I have to say about the gender pay gap.

There are ways to boost your confidence and we share those in the final section of this chapter. However, it may not be as simple as that. Bowles et al. (2007) explore how women and men respond when initiating negotiations for financial reward. Rather than a focus on 'fixing the women' to make them more confident, Bowles argues that 'gender based norms of appropriate behaviour may influence whether individuals decide to negotiate' (2007: 100). Women may be reluctant to negotiate because they feel that this may have a detrimental impact for them in the organisation for which they work and 'the social cost of negotiating for pay is not significant for men, while it *is* significant for women' (emphasis in original) (Bowles, 2014). Do women lack the confidence to discuss a salary increase or do they feel that initiating a discussion is likely to penalise them in the eyes of their line manager? Unconscious bias strikes again.

IT'S COMPLEX!

You are working very hard and for long hours doing the absolute best that you can. Yet, as a woman, there are related factors that work against you earning the same as a man doing a similar job. How would you answer these questions?

A MALE PRIMARY HEADTEACHER

Are male primary headteachers earning £1,700 a year more, on average, because they are more effective at running larger schools and so are higher up the pay range than women? Or are women deputy headteachers in primary schools unable to find a part-time leadership role which would ensure they returned after parental leave and eventually became a headteacher? Or do members of the headteacher appraisal panel award large salary increases because their unconscious bias wants to retain a man as so few apply?

A FEMALE SECONDARY HEADTEACHER

Are female secondary headteachers earning £700 a year less because they underestimate their own ability and do not ask for a larger salary when first appointed? Or are senior women leaders opting out of applying for headships because they feel the role is incompatible with their personal circumstances? Or are more men appointed as secondary headteachers because unconscious bias influences the male and female members of the appointment panel to choose the male image of a leader?

The gender gap exists due to a complicated mesh of individual, organisational and systemic challenges as depicted on the graphic for the #WomenEd value that underpins this chapter, that of challenge. Let's see what can bring about the change that is needed.

HOW CAN WE REDUCE AND ERADICATE THE GENDER PAY GAP?

AS INDIVIDUALS

As women, we must understand that so many of our thoughts and actions are the result of 'socialization and stereotyping' (Fuller, 2017 citing Cubillo and Brown, 2003). We can acknowledge and accept this. We can learn new beliefs and think something bold. I love a tweet by Helena Morrisey (2018) who says,

> The data should not be used as an excuse to beat up the companies with the worst GPGs [Gender Pay Gaps] – see the data in

the context of both sector and society – but we need real action plans. We cannot fix the past but we can write the future.

The pay gap data only tells us what is happening now. We can 'write the future', we can empower ourselves to choose what is right. So:

- know that you have worth
- know you can achieve your next leadership step if you choose to do so
- find your own way to celebrate your achievements, especially at work

NEGOTIATE

Negotiating skills can be useful for many opportunities: a pay increase or to work flexibly; request more free time or administrative support. Remember that you are excellent at what you do, accept it is uncomfortable and difficult and do it anyway. Practice makes perfect apparently, and this is a fabulous mantra for all the perfectionists reading this!

Try this!

A new employer

- If you want a job with a *new employer*, remember, it's cost them time and money to find you, they want you to work with them
- Say thank you, that you are keen to accept subject to the salary, ask for an offer in writing which includes the suggested salary and say you will get back to them quickly
- As soon as you get the offer, say you want to join them though you are hesitating about the salary
- See what they say. If it's not enough, ask if they can go higher. Remind them of your passion and expertise and remember it will cost them to recruit again
- If they are adamant they can't go higher, and you want the job, ask about other elements that would help you, for example, a costed professional learning opportunity

An internal post, or for a salary increase

- Remember it would cost your employer a lot of time and money to replace you
- Make sure your interviewers or your line manager know about specific examples of your achievements, the benefit you bring to the organisation, and that you're already doing work of a higher level. Remember me when I was offered the headteacher post! Offer to send your suggestion about the role or salary in writing as a little time can help people to think. Then follow the steps from above
- If they still say no, ask what you need to do to gain an increase or a promotion in the next 6 or 12 months

If you want to request flexible working, have a look at Chapter 10. It's important to do your research thoroughly and present a business case that would benefit both you and your organisation.

Negotiating may take you out of your comfort zone, so then it's about being 10% braver. It's also about tackling the confidence gap by remembering that you are as competent and capable as others – in fact, downright amazing.

Most importantly, women need to *apply* for leadership roles. A McKinsey report (Barsh et al., 2008) highlighted that one of the most powerful forces holding women back is their own self-limiting beliefs and the unconscious or conscious bias of both male and female leaders. Women need to take the risk and apply for more leadership roles and so learn from the feedback if the job wasn't for them.

If your confidence level is still low, try what I do. I remember that women are very good at faking things. I'm talking about our hair colour, our shape, our skin. I'm very fair so in the summer I slap on false tan to feel better. Slap on the false confidence and, even if you don't feel it, project confidence and be 10% braver. It's a little bit of magic.

AGITATE FOR CHANGE

- If your organisation has published a gender pay gap, ask them how they will reduce the gap year on year. Offer to work with them on creating the plan and evaluating progress
- If your organisation didn't have to publish a gender pay gap, ask them to do it anyway. Ask senior leaders to think about diversity as well as gender in their plans
- Review your flexible working strategy or work with others, including governors/trustees to develop one
- Ask senior leaders about offering crèche facilities
- Connect with your #WomenEd team and host an event in your locality
- Include your students in the work you do in this area; it's their future even more than ours
- And a difficult one! Think about who does parental and caring responsibilities with your partner so that you share these

ORGANISATIONAL PERSPECTIVES

The most important advice is to lead from the top. According to McKinsey (Barsh et al., 2008), only systemic change can make a real difference to your culture, processes and practice. As the UK is in the grip of a recruitment and retention crisis, senior leaders should make an organisational and a moral case to support more women into leadership posts.

- Review your culture, practice and processes to see how you can improve your support for women to be leaders – involve women in this process
- Check your own gender pay gap and if your organisation didn't need to report in 2018, then do it. Let women know you want to do this as you think it is important and involve them
- Create a development plan to reduce your gender pay gap year on year
- Review your recruitment materials, avoid gendered language and consider making them blind

- Remove the request for a current salary from your recruitment materials
- Review or develop a flexible working strategy
- Offer crèche facilities on your own or with partners
- Offer all jobs as flexible, part time or a job share unless there is a strong business case not to
- Encourage new fathers to take their parental leave and normalise this

CHANGING THE SYSTEM

At current rates of progress, it will take 100 years to close the gender pay gap (Fawcett Society, n.d.). To eradicate their gender pay gap, Iceland is the first country to legislate that employers must *prove* they pay everyone equally, no matter their gender, ethnicity or sexuality. Iceland is also ranked first in *The Global Gender Gap Report 2016* by the World Economic Forum.

The gender pay gap is widest for older women but the UK saw a widening of the pay gap for younger women in November 2017, which suggests we are going backwards. To eradicate the gender pay gap, systemic change is needed. We look forward to women in education being valued for their leadership contribution and paid a salary that is equal to their worth.

QUESTIONS

- In what ways does this chapter reflect or resonate with your experience?
- Do you have a personal gender gap? If so, what will you do to reduce this gap?
- What will you pledge to do to ensure women leaders in your organisation are paid equitably when compared to their male counterparts?
- How will you agitate for systemic change?

ROLE MODEL: STELLA CREASY

Stella Creasy was re-elected as Labour MP for Walthamstow on 7 May 2015, taking 68.9% of the vote. She has been the MP for Walthamstow since 2010 and is a member of the Labour Women's Network. Stella stood as a candidate in the Labour Party deputy leadership election in 2015 and came second with 26% of the vote. As a councillor she was the Mayor, Deputy Mayor and Chief Whip during her time serving the people of Waltham Forest. Stella gained a PhD in psychology and won the 2005 Richard Titmuss Prize at the London School of Economics.

I chose Stella as my role model because in April 2018, she, and a group of cross-party women MPs, set up #PayMeToo to ensure women earn what they deserve (Creasy,

(Continued)

(Continued)

2018). In the article she wrote to launch this campaign, she took Ryanair to task: 'Ryanair defends having a gender pay gap of 72% by pointing out how few women are pilots and how many are cabin crew. Their chief executive claims it is a "feature" of the airline industry, as though a penis is required to be able to fly a plane.' I love this quotation because I also think that genitalia should not affect pay. I hope that all women educators will continue to argue this until the pay gap has disappeared.

REFERENCES

Adams, A. and Duncan, P. (2018) 'Gender pay gaps in academy school chains among the worst in UK', *The Guardian*, 25 March [Online]. Available at: www.theguardian.com/news/2018/mar/25/gender-pay-gaps-in-academy-school-chains-among-the-worst-in-uk (accessed 4 April 2018).

Allen, R. (2018) 'Four reasons why female teachers are paid less than men'. Institute of Education blog, June [Online]. Available at: https://ioelondonblog.wordpress.com/2018/06/21/four-reasons-why-female-teachers-are-paid-less-than-men/ (accessed 8 July 2018).

Babcock, L. and Laschever, S. (n.d.) *Women Don't Ask* [Online]. Available at: www.womendontask.com/stats.html (accessed 8 July 2018).

Babcock, L., Laschever, S., Gelfand, M. and Small, D. (2003) 'Nice girls don't ask,' *Harvard Business Review*, October [Online]. Available at: https://hbr.org/2003/10/nice-girls-dont-ask (accessed 30 May 2018).

Barsh, J., Cranston, S. and Craske, R. (2008) 'Centered leadership: How talented women thrive', *McKinsey Quarterly*, May [Online]. Available at: www.mckinsey.com/global-themes/leadership/centered-leadership-how-talented-women-thrive (accessed 18 April 2018).

BBC (2018a) 'Why do schools have a massive pay gap?', *BBC News*, 20 March [Online]. Available at: www.bbc.co.uk/news/education-43460998 (accessed 8 July 2018).

BBC (2018b) 'Worst universities' gender pay gap in England is 37%', *BBC News*, 5 April [Online]. Available at: www.bbc.co.uk/news/uk-england-43655192 (accessed 8 March 2018).

Bowles, H. (2014) 'Why women don't negotiate their job offers,' *Harvard Business Review*, 19 June [Online]. Available at: https://hbr.org/2014/06/why-women-dont-negotiate-their-job-offers (accessed 30 May 2018).

Bowles, H.R., Babcock, L. and Lai, L. (2007) 'Social incentives for gender differences in the propensity to initiate negotiations: Sometimes it does hurt to ask', *Organizational Behavior and Human Decision Processes*, 103(1): 84–103.

Cecchi-Dimeglio, P. (2017) 'How gender bias corrupts performance reviews, and what to do about it', *Harvard Business Review*, 12 April [Online]. Available at: https://hbr.org/2017/04/how-gender-bias-corrupts-performance-reviews-and-what-to-do-about-it (accessed 18 May 2018).

Corell, S., Benard, S. and Pail, I. (2007) 'Getting a job: Is there a motherhood penalty?', *American Journal of Sociology*, 112(5): 1297–1339.

Creasy, S. (2018) 'We've set up #PayMeToo to ensure women earn what they deserve', *The Guardian*, 4 April [Online]. Available at: www.theguardian.com/commentisfree/2018/apr/04/paymetoo-women-earn-gender-pay-gap-action (accessed 6 April 2018).

Department for Education (DfE) (2018) *School Leadership in England*. London: DfE.

Education Datalab (2015) 'Women dominate the teaching profession, but men are winning the pay game', in *Seven Things You Might Not Know About Our Schools* (pp. 24–27) [Online]. Available at: https://ffteducationdatalab.org.uk/wp-content/uploads/2016/02/EduDataLab-7things.pdf (accessed 8 July 2018).

Fawcett Society (n.d.) *Close the Gender Pay Gap* [Online]. Available at: www.fawcettsociety.org.uk/close-gender-pay-gap (accessed 8 July 2018).

Fuller, K. (2017) 'Women secondary head teachers in England: Where are they now?', *Management in Education*, *31*(2): 54–68.

Glass, J. (2004) 'Blessing or curse? Work-family policies and mothers' wage growth over time', *Work and Occupations*, *31*: 367–394

Heilman, M. (2001) 'Description and prescription: How gender stereotypes prevent women's ascent up the organizational ladder', *Journal of Social Issues*, *57*(4): 657–674.

House of Commons Women and Equalities Committee (2016) *Gender Pay Gap*, Second Report of Session 2015–16. Available at: https://publications.parliament.uk/pa/cm201516/cmselect/cmwomeq/584/584.pdf (accessed 14 May 2018).

Institute for Fiscal Studies (2018) *Mothers Suffer Long-term Pay Penalty from Part-time Working*, IFS, 5 February [Online]. Available at: www.ifs.org.uk/publications/10364 (accessed 18 May 2018).

Kay, K. and Shipman, C. (2014) 'The confidence gap', *The Atlantic*, May [Online]. Available at: www.theatlantic.com/magazine/archive/2014/05/the-confidence-gap/359815/ (accessed 6 May 2018).

Mansell, W. (2016) 'The academy male chiefs of the future? Largely white and very male', *The Guardian*, 12 April [Online]. Available at: www.theguardian.com/education/2016/apr/12/multi-academy-trusts-chiefs-primary-schools-david-carter (accessed 24 April 2018).

Morrisey, H. [@MorriseyHelena] (2018) 4 April [Tweet]. Available at: https://twitter.com/MorriseyHelena/status/981447600107868160 (accessed 4 April 2018).

Moss-Racusin, C., Dovidiob, J., Brescoll V., Graham M. and Handelsmana, J. (2012) 'Science faculty's subtle gender biases favor male students', Proceedings of the National Academy of Sciences of the United States of America (PNAS), 9 October [Online]. Available at: www.pnas.org/content/109/41/16474 (accessed 8 July 2018).

Nye, P. (2018) *The Gender Pay Gap in Academy Trusts*, Education Datalab blog, 3 April [Online]. Available at: https://educationdatalab.org.uk/2018/04/the-gender-pay-gap-in-academy-trusts/ (accessed 14 April 2018).

Portman, N. (2015) *Harvard Commencement Speech*. Available at: www.youtube.com/watch?v=jDaZu_KEMCY (accessed 14 April 2018).

Pounders, J. and Coleman, M. (2002) 'Women – better leaders than men? In general and educational management it still "all depends"', *Leadership & Organization Development Journal*, *23*(3): 122–133.

Simons, J. (ed.) (2016) *The Importance of Teachers: A Collection of Essays on Teacher Recruitment and Retention*. Policy Exchange. Available at: https://policyexchange.org.uk/wp-content/uploads/2016/09/the-Importance-of-Teachers.pdf (accessed 5 May 2018).

Staufenberg, C. (2018) 'Investigation: The ups and downs of academy CEO pay', *Schools Week*, 22 May [Online]. Available at: https://schoolsweek.co.uk/investigation-the-ups-and-downs-of-academy-ceo-pay/ (accessed 14 April 2018).

Taylor, S.E., Fiske, S.T., Etcoff, N.L. and Ruderman, A.J. (1978) 'Categorical and contextual bases of person memory and stereotyping', *Journal of Personality and Social Psychology*, *36*(7): 778–793.

Topping, A., Barr, C. and Duncan, P. (2018) 'Gender pay gap figures reveal eight in 10 UK firms pay men more', *The Guardian*, 4 April [Online]. Available at: www.theguardian.com/money/2018/apr/04/gender-pay-gap-figures-reveal-eight-in-10-uk-firms-pay-men-more (accessed 4 July 2018).

University and College Union (UCU) (2017) *The Gender Pay Gap in Higher Education 2015/16 Data Report*. London: UCU.

Ward, H. (2018) 'More female staff but less equal pay – the sorry state of our schools', *Tes*, 30 March [Online]. Available at: www.tes.com/news/tes-magazine/tes-magazine/more-female-staff-less-equal-pay-sorry-state-our-schools (accessed 4 July 2018).

World Economic Forum (2016) *The Global Gender Gap Report 2016* [Online]. Available at: http://reports.weforum.org/global-gender-gap-report-2016/rankings/ (accessed 17 July 2018).

12

STILL WE RISE: OUR AGENDA FOR THE FUTURE

KEZIAH FEATHERSTONE

KEY POINTS

This chapter will:

- Reflect on the overall impact of all we have achieved so far

- Consider what more needs to be achieved and how we can do this together

- Draw our future agenda together under the banner of our eight core values

- Suggest how you can contribute and be part of the journey

INTRODUCTION

Within a very short space of time, and without any grand plan, #WomenEd has exploded onto the educational landscape. In Chapter 1, Hannah celebrates our many successes, yet there remain substantial pockets of scepticism and resistance. Certainly, the general landscape for women in education has not yet changed; our impact remains relatively individual and localised.

It does not help that in many places there is a drive to homogenise school leadership; parts of the system celebrate the bland, the routine, the tested. To call oneself a feminist can be construed as radicalisation and to actively seek the improvement of women's lives as unnecessary. It is as if the very foundations of the English establishment have been transformed.

History suggests to us that the greatest early teachers were men like Plato, Socrates, Aristotle; women were carers, wives, mothers, goddesses ... When women began to enter the teaching workforce *en masse* around the late nineteenth century, a plethora of rules were laid upon the profession, mostly to ensure women's roles were about proper conduct and servitude, not pedagogy or improving outcomes for children.

We've seen documents such as the USA's Rules for Teachers from both 1872 and 1915, although the accuracy of these cannot be fully verified; today we just laugh at the notion of having to wear two petticoats and to be home by eight p.m. (*Open Culture*, 2013).

However, certainly in the 1920s when so many men were unemployed in the UK, action was taken to move women out of the classroom via a 'marriage bar' that banned married women from working as teachers and was not lifted until 1944. Indeed, Rhondda Education Authority in July 1922 dismissed 63 married women teachers; when the women took the local authority to court, they lost their case (BBC, 2011). This was despite the Sex Disqualification Removal Act that was passed in 1919.

Even with anti-discriminatory legislation in place, women were discriminated against. Just because there is a law against it doesn't mean, even now, that women will be treated fairly.

And, as Claire Nicholls argues in Chapter 7, there is a lasting belief that men have a place among the intellectual positions and women in the nurturing roles, even to the detriment of men who wish to pursue a teaching career. The headline in *The Telegraph* (Paton, 2018) of 'Teaching in primary schools "still seen as a woman's job"' was amplified to 'Men are being put off applying for jobs in primary schools because working with young children is seen as a "woman's profession", according to research.'

Essentially, there is so much more to do and we are working together to achieve this.

CLARITY

Are we all clear now that there is a gender imbalance in education? Interestingly, there has been a minority of voices that dispute this. Voices that claim they know plenty of women leaders, so what if it is a bit lopsided? Voices that say women don't want to be leaders. Voices that claim women often choose to remain in the classroom, or go part time because of their families, as if that is the answer, rather than being another barrier. Other male voices that could be raised in vociferous support follow our community silently, uncertain of the reaction of others. We wish they would join our #HeForShe advocates as Chris Hildrew has done (see Chapter 9) and as some men do on Twitter.

Our ongoing responsibility has been and will continue to be the unpicking of what exactly is happening for women leaders in education and why. A great deal of the data that we observe is noisy. As Sameena explored in Chapter 5, issues around intersectionality make things extremely challenging for many women affected by layers upon layers of (un)conscious bias.

We must continue to make the problems women face very clear and also identify achievable ways to address them. This book is just the start.

As well as our own organisational clarity, I see our longer term purpose to be to support other women to have clarity in what they want to achieve. Unless women know and understand all the possible routes open to them and how to open routes up that aren't so accessible for them, fewer will wish to travel. What is it that each person wishes to achieve in their life and their career? How can we support them to articulate it with absolute clarity so that their ambition can become a plan and the plan a reality?

In Chapter 8, Jill identified some brilliant strategies for getting that next job and also doing all that can be done to be successful at it. However, we are also mindful that personal drive and ambition, let alone ability, do not always ensure success.

With this in mind, we also need complete clarity about what we want our schools to be like. We have to ensure that the cultures being fostered and celebrated are those that are family friendly and open to flexible ways of working, where home–work life balances are developed. We need genuine meritocracies where values are not laminated posters, but agreed on and put into practice by all those in the institution.

Clarity must never be assumed. Several high profile commentators have been critical of our flexible working campaign. When quizzed, it was because they had assumed that #WomenEd was promoting part-time working as a solution to teacher workload. Absolutely not. Never should anyone have to choose to be paid to work fewer days simply so they can get through their marking and planning. Although we had assumed our position was obvious, it clearly wasn't.

With the largest demographic leaving teaching being women in their thirties, addressing the recruitment and retention crisis facing our schools requires the vast majority of those in leadership positions to understand the issues facing women leaders and adapt existing practice. This is something we will continue to work towards.

COMMUNICATION

We have to keep promoting the #WomenEd mission relentlessly in as many ways as possible. We are a movement born on social media and our infant years have been characterised by celebrating the growing number of people who connect with us, whilst also skirmishing online with naysayers. Frankly, it is frustrating. But it is worth persevering as every time we restate our beliefs, we connect with new people. Our communication reach grows.

Hannah confessed in the opening chapter that we had no clear communication strategy at the beginning. Ironically, for strategic leaders, we approached everything in a rather haphazard way. So it is with education sometimes. The wider purpose can seem so urgent, so important, that we simply want to communicate without considering *how* this is done.

Key means of communication such as the #WomenEd blog did not come online until our third year. One of the reasons for this was our use of the third-party blogging site Staffrm, which enabled many early voices to be heard. Why invest time in an alternative whilst Staffrm was working so well? It was not until Staffrm could no longer continue that we looked at an alternative to meet the needs of our community. The future has to be adaptive and flexible.

Clearly one of the most important ways we will communicate in future starts with *this* book. For the first time, and in a significant way, a solid artefact will be held in the hands of a wider community. For those working in education with no desire or means to connect on social media, we will be able to show who we are and what we do. In the twenty-first century what can a book do that a blog or website can't? It lends credence to the message and to the size of our audience, and it will most certainly connect with people who have no idea who we are yet.

Our approach to communication has been generously supported by several high-profile editors of national publications: Alice Woolley, of *Education Guardian*; Ann Mroz, of *Tes* Laura McInerney and Shane Mann of *Schools Week*. With these publications amplifying the #WomenEd voice both in print and online, we have been able to reach new people. Rather than being a bit of a radicalised, fringe group, we are being asked for comment as mainstream representatives.

In terms of the future, no one form of communication will cover everything we wish to achieve. We communicate in person through #LeadMeets (informal after-school gatherings where people share leadership tips, advice and stories); through the larger unconferences and through smaller and informal social gatherings. @WomenEdSW ran an experiment during the summer of 2017 to operate application letter workshops, where women brought their letters of application with them for feedback. It is something that could have been done on the phone or via email, like much coaching, but the face-to-face connection amplifies the support and high regard we have for one another. Such opportunities have to continue and grow, rather than be replaced by something akin to internet banking. We will always be first and foremost for the people in our community.

CONNECTION

Unless we focus on connecting existing and aspiring women leaders, and those who support them, the movement will become a vacuous echo chamber. In the same way as our communication has to be both in person and virtual, so our connections need to be both.

Over the past few years #WomenEd has attended many established UK educational events and conferences: Wellington Festival of Education, Northern Rocks, Inspiring Leadership (Association of School and College Leaders (ASCL)/National Association of Head Teachers (NAHT)), The Schools, Students and Teachers' Network (SSAT) Conference. Through the kind hosting of these organisations, we have been able to connect and grow our community. Additional women have heard about us, men have vowed to support us, and those organisations have noted the power of our message.

When the Department for Education hosted two workforce summits in 2017/18, one on flexible working and one on diversity, #WomenEd were invited to the policy table. We appreciate that for true impact to be seen here we may need to wait, albeit impatiently. However, we do consider the urgency that people feel to invite us to such events as evidence of potential impact. The need to consider gender matters as part of the everyday discourse has become essential, not an add-on.

We are working with a wider group of people and organisations than ever before. It was particularly pleasing that, at the 2018 Wellington Festival of Education, Vivienne was joined for her session on the gender pay gap by Professor Rebecca Allen, who was able to present additional information and data around the premise that women are like men, only cheaper.

Our growing connections can sometimes be tested, so although we wish them to continue to grow we need to also ensure everyone understands our mission and our values. We have, on occasion, been approached by companies wishing to sponsor an event, or support free childcare, or cover catering costs. Goodness knows we value such support given we are a not-for-profit organisation run by volunteers, but upon further investigation we occasionally learn that their own values are completely opposite to ours. For them, throwing some money at #WomenEd, being able to feature in the same event, buys them the illusion of something they don't really understand but know will bring them a wider audience. We prefer to trust that our values are so clear that only like-minded organisations wish to collaborate with us and we are steely minded if we realise our trust is misplaced. As our community grows at a fast pace, I believe that in the future we need to consider how to sustain and protect such trust.

The connection with men is essential but problematic. Our mission is clear. #WomenEd is for women, we all work in schools with men, we often live with men and men are frequently those making leadership appointments. Not only does Chris explore the #HeforShe agenda brilliantly in Chapter 9, he also provides some excellent strategies for how men in schools can support women. None of us want anyone to charge on a shining horse to the princess' rescue as Jules describes in Chapter 3. These damsels are hardly in distress and they can sort things out for themselves, thank you very much. However, the playing field is not currently level; there is too much institutionalised bias; too many barriers not of our own making to overcome. Only with the support of men can we make progress as fast as we wish. And the vast majority of women, who choose to work in a feminised workforce for the benefit of children everywhere, only agree with this.

Men, don't be shy. Don't stand on ceremony and never be worried about making mistakes. Wave, wade, squeeze, smile your way in: we will all benefit.

COMMUNITY

Our community has to grow; it has to be diverse and inclusive of everyone. Whilst maintaining our mission of supporting current and aspiring women to be leaders in education, we have to consider who those women are in as wide a way as possible. We must include the teaching assistants, the initial teacher trainee, the newly qualified teacher and the chief executives and the politicians who advocate for us. Men who are happy and willing to support this mission are also part of the community. The community must welcome those of all faiths, backgrounds, ethnicities, nationalities, those with disabilities, those who are a part of the LGBQT+ community and, frankly, anyone else who wishes to join us.

As Claire Nicholls explored, some sectors of education are more feminised than others, such as early years, and special schools. We must hear their voices as loudly as those working in secondary schools or higher education. Importantly we need to hear these voices to bust some of the myths around working in these sectors.

Not everyone in the community agrees with one another; even the co-founders don't always agree with one another! But this is good. Rigorous and respectful discourse is the bedrock of democracy. We are a democratic community; for example our fourth unconference had an open call to offer to facilitate. This brought in nearly 80 volunteers, all offering a workshop or presentation. Instead of the steering group choosing the final line-up, this was voted on by the regional leaders, those most closely attuned to the wishes of our local communities. Given that we also held the fourth unconference in its fourth location around the UK, we are determined to continue reaching out to the community wherever it is.

COLLABORATION

#WomenEd will only strengthen if we collaborate with other people and organisations. We have to model ways of working we advocate for schools and individuals. Whether we are trying to make something like co-headship far more widely known and considered, or schools are sharing brilliant staff in order to retain them, we also reflect on which collaborations will benefit our community.

At two separate ends of the profession, Professor Sam Twiselton OBE, expert in initial teacher training, and Dame Alison Peacock, CEO of the Chartered College of Teaching (CCoT), have both been extraordinarily supportive of #WomenEd.

Sam clearly articulates the need for all new entrants to the profession to consider their longer term impact; she references many great organisations to facilitate this, including #WomenEd. Her ongoing support led to the third unconference in 2017 being held at Sheffield Hallam University and welcoming keynotes by Jo Miller and Jackie Drayton from local government to add to the delegates' understanding of the wider context for our children and their families.

Alison is an equally strong advocate of #WomenEd. We have sought to recommend membership of CCoT to our members and were delighted when Vivienne and Hannah became Founding Fellows in 2018. Hannah was then elected to the Council of the College and Vivienne was elected Vice President. We believe this mutual relationship can strengthen both organisations and, with the CCoT including leadership in its remit, we see our partnership growing, especially with regard to supporting women's leadership and flexible working.

Likewise, co-founders Helena Marsh (Chapter 10) and I are now part of the Headteachers' Roundtable, a non-political think tank that aims to influence educational policy. This sort of collaboration does not split us in two; we never find ourselves torn between two ideologies. Rather, they complement and support one another; the voices amplify rather than diminish them. On matters around accountability, recruitment and retention, and the curriculum, we are able to offer a different perspective. For example, the gender pay gap may well start in early years with stereotyped play, or when options are taken at the age of 14. How can we improve the female uptake of STEM subjects when they occupy such a small part of the primary curriculum in favour of content for the all-consuming standard assessment tests?

In the coming years, I would like to see #WomenEd work more collaboratively with the unions representing people working in schools: teachers' unions, leaders' unions and unions representing support staff. We have been fortunate to be championed by ASCL's Geoff Barton, NAHT's Nick Brook and the National Education Union's (NEU) Dr Mary Bousted and Kevin Courtney – clearly they understand the need to embrace all women in the profession.

However, when much of the discrimination facing women comes from employers, I hope further collaboration could help to prevent discrimination arising in the first place. Not everyone who works in a school is expertly conversant with employment law, including those who hire and, occasionally, fire. For example, too frequently a woman returning from maternity leave will meet with her headteacher to be told she has to rescind her leadership position if she wishes to go part time. Is this really lawful, we ask? How can we equip those going into such a meeting with all the information needed to ensure a positive outcome for all? It may be difficult to timetable part-time teachers, but it is a far better option than losing good staff and spending a fortune to replace them.

At the end of the day, the wider picture has to be about making children's education the best it can be and schools need the best teachers to achieve this.

CONFIDENCE

There is nothing inherent in a woman's physiology to predispose her to a lack of confidence. Confidence is not, like cheese, something that comes gendered (see Jules' Chapter 3). However, the qualitative data, the anecdotes, the stories being shared at events reveal a confidence gap. It is not binary. There are plenty of confident women in the workforce and plenty of men lack confidence too. But for a significant sector of women in education, their response to their lack of confidence holds them back, and for many reasons, confidence is a significant block.

Shared at the first unconference in 2015, one woman revealed how she had remained a deputy head for 11 years before 'getting the guts' to apply for her first headship. She didn't get the job and it knocked her so much that she didn't apply for another one for a further seven years. Given that she took over the role of deputy from a male member of staff who had remained in the role for just 18 months before applying for promotion, the difference can be quite stark.

Vivienne's Chapter 11 on the gender pay gap thoroughly explores the inequity in factors that affect pay. These factors also affect us when it comes to whether or not we apply for jobs as well as how we perform when in post. If we perceive that a job is only available to us if we can work full time, or need to put unfathomable hours into the role, or have to espouse 'sporting values' or exude 'gravitas', then we are unlikely to have the confidence to apply and fight to change the nature of the job being advertised whilst we're actually mid-interview.

Employers must recognise that, often, they unconsciously erect barriers that prevent many women from applying in the first place. In Louise Tickle's excellent article 'Language in school job ads puts women off headteacher roles' (2018), Vivienne explored how simply changing the vocabulary used in job adverts could revolutionise how accessible women view more leadership roles. As Vivienne explained, 'It's just not how they see themselves or how they want to do leadership when they get there'.

Not only do we need to continue advocating a change of language use in adverts, we also need to support women to apply for these jobs regardless. There is every chance the real job bears little resemblance to the macho position in the advert, after all. Perhaps the wording of the advert is clumsy rather than intentional. Regardless, apply! Things have changed since Claire Cuthbert's experience, as shared by Angie Browne in Chapter 6, haven't they?

Gender and confidence is a much bigger issue than #WomenEd: it is a global concern and affects nearly every aspect of world culture. Liz Free corroborates this in Chapter 4 when she describes the synergy of concerns expressed across four of our international teams. It is many centuries of embedded misogyny and mistrust and won't vanish overnight. That's why we have to call it out, articulate it and offer solutions and support.

Indeed, there was scarcely a woman we approached to contribute a chapter to this book who didn't undergo some degree of 'imposter syndrome', either initially or whilst writing. Even now, as with Vivienne in Chapter 11, I am thinking *who in the world will read my words and not think I'm ridiculous?* I'm not without ego myself. A two-time headteacher, in education for nearly 25 years, I've spoken on platforms to thousands of people and published many articles. And yet my confidence level is inexplicably low and so is that of so many women I know. It has to change.

CHALLENGE

Education is all about challenge. We challenge ourselves, one another, the children, their families and the communities in which they grow up. If it isn't challenging, there is no learning to be done. To avoid challenge in education for ourselves, or the children, is a form of poverty, of lack. It isn't acceptable.

And so that should also be the way we challenge ourselves professionally. After reading Louise Tickle's article, mentioned above, long-time #WomenEd advocate and headteacher Vic Goddard tweeted that he'd found it personally challenging to read. He ended up needing to clarify that he wasn't personally challenging the assertion put forward; rather, he had felt challenged reading it as, quite often, *he* is that male leader being asked for in such adverts.

In many ways, agreeing with particular #WomenEd arguments is not as important as engaging with them. When reading us, or listening to us, taking on board potentially challenging concepts is extremely brave. The openness and humility to engage with something that challenges our fundamental identity or beliefs is to be celebrated. Using one's privilege, whether as a man, or as a white person, or a heterosexual person, to challenge a hegemony that benefits us is the ultimate challenge.

10% Braver is not a glib slogan. When Sue Cowley said it at our first unconference, as she retells in Chapter 2, it passed me by a little. But it has grown with the movement, with each of us. What it now means to me is not what it means to you. However, if you are being braver than you have been before, you're also definitely challenging yourself. Be braver for yourself and for one another.

CHANGE

#WomenEd has to be about change. Too much needs to be put right simply to describe it and then leave it be.

We want to change ourselves, as women and as educators. For some of us, we want to change the impact we have on the world, the difference we make to children's lives and the schools we can shape.

We want to change one another in whatever ways others wish to be changed. It has to be consensual! We want to change the way people are treated in schools and whether they're welcomed into those schools in the first place.

We know that the ridiculous divisions between men and women, between boys and girls, between teachers and leaders, between early years, primary, secondary, further and higher education, need to go. Divisions between state schools and independents, between faith schools and those that are secular, between mainstream and special or alternative provision do nothing to help children and educators. Within the #WomenEd community we work collaboratively for change, for clarity in communication, and we challenge ourselves to find the confidence to do this.

Drs Kay Fuller and Jill Berry secured funding to conduct research into the early impact of #WomenEd through the University of Nottingham. Asked to summarise what the research conducted so far indicates for the future of #WomenEd, Kay writes in a way that I feel closes this chapter of our story perfectly:

> #WomenEd is achieving something we have needed in many countries for a long time. A network of women provides nurturance, support and challenge for one another as educators, serving and aspiring leaders, support staff and volunteers in education. [Our research] . . . shows women value the positive mindset of #WomenEd. They are aware of structural, organisational and individual barriers to women in formal leadership positions but the connections established via social media and reinforced at events mean women are being nurtured, supported and challenged by colleagues beyond their institutions. There is a real cross-fertilisation of ideas through relationships building across the system. (Personal communication, 2017)

As for the future, all the men and half the women interviewed by Fuller and Berry recognised a need for gender equity education. #WomenEd has a role to play in ensuring equity as well as excellence is in the curriculum. That goes for an intersectional approach to focus on race equality as well as equality for women and men regardless of sexual orientation, age, disability, religion and social class.

There remains a long way to go to establish gender equity in our workplaces and society, but education is a good place to start. We look forward to being 10% braver alongside you.

ROLE MODELS: FEMALE MPS

To truly understand what women have to face when they step forward in the name of public service, I draw your attention to the research undertaken by Amnesty International after the 2017 UK Election.

I doubt many were that surprised to discover that the UK's first black female MP, Diane Abbott, is most relentlessly targeted: 'She receives an incredibly disproportionate amount of abuse and was the target of almost a third (31.61%) of all abusive tweets we analysed. She received even more abuse in the six weeks leading up to 2017's snap general election, when 45.14% of abusive tweets were aimed at her.'

With most of the tweets being misogynistic and/or racist, and with so many threatening violence, including rape, it would be easy to imagine Ms Abbott simply wanting to give up. With around 50 such abusive texts *per day* being sent to one woman, her courage and strength makes her a role model for many of us.

She is not alone, although she stands out by a long margin. Amnesty International note that 'The disproportionate amount of online abuse faced by BAME women MPs reflects a wider trend of "intersectional discrimination", i.e. that which targets an individual on the basis of their different identities, such as their race, gender, class, sexual orientation, etc' (Amnesty International, 2017).

So, the intersectional discrimination faced by women teachers, as explored by Sameena in Chapter 5, is replicated here.

Other women MPs more commonly singled out include Emily Thornbury and Jess Phillips from Labour, the Conservative's Anna Soubry and Joanna Cherry of the Scottish Nationalist Party.

Hearteningly, some of these women MPs are among those who have put aside party political allegiances to work together for women's rights in Parliament. The morning after a packed-out reception in the House of Commons to celebrate 100 years since the first women in the UK got the vote, Jess Phillips said, 'More than ever it feels like women make the agenda,' and the #WomenEd community cheered to hear 'I think across the country, actually, our voices have got louder' (Silver, 2018).

Therefore, these women MPs, who have banded together despite all the abuse directed at them, and regardless of political badge, are my role models. Sometimes getting together to make a change is, by far, the bigger priority.

CHANGING THE SYSTEM

- When looking at your institution's leadership team, how equal or diverse would the children themselves see it? Do they see themselves in the leadership of the school? If they do not, what can be actively done to improve this?

- How can you, and others you encourage, contribute to the future agenda of #WomenEd?

- What will the educational landscape look like when #WomenEd's mission is accomplished?

REFERENCES

Amnesty International UK (2017) *Black and Asian Women MPs Abused More Online* [Online]. Available at: www.amnesty.org.uk/online-violence-women-mps (accessed 10 May 2018).

BBC (2011) 'Women and teaching', *BBC Wales History*, 10 March [Online]. Available at: www.bbc.co.uk/wales/history/sites/themes/society/women_teaching.shtml (accessed 5 May 2018).

Fuller, K. (2018) Direct message on Twitter to the author (15 April). Personal communication.

Open Culture (2013) 'Rules for teachers in 1872 and 1915: No drinking, smoking, or trips to barber shops and ice cream parlors', *Open Culture*, 16 September [Online]. Available at: www.openculture.com/2013/09/rules-for-teachers-in-1872-1915-no-drinking-smoking-or-trips-to-barber-shops-and-ice-cream-parlors.html (accessed 5 May 2018).

Paton, G. (2018) 'Teaching in primary schools "still seen as a woman's job"', *The Telegraph*, 17 September [Online]. Available at: www.telegraph.co.uk/education/educationnews/9849976/Teaching-in-primary-schools-still-seen-as-a-womans-job.html (accessed 27 May 2018).

Silver, L. (2018) 'Here's how some MPs have put aside party politics to force change on women's issues', *BuzzFeedNews*, March [Online]. Available at: www.buzzfeed.com/laurasilver/these-women-mps-have-put-aside-party-politics-to-get? (accessed 18 May 2018).

Tickle, L. (2018) 'Language in school job ads puts women off headteacher roles', *The Guardian*, 19 June [Online]. Available at: www.theguardian.com/education/2018/jun/19/language-school-headteacher-job-ads-puts-women-off (accessed 20 June 2018).

INDEX